The DJ Handbook

Second edition

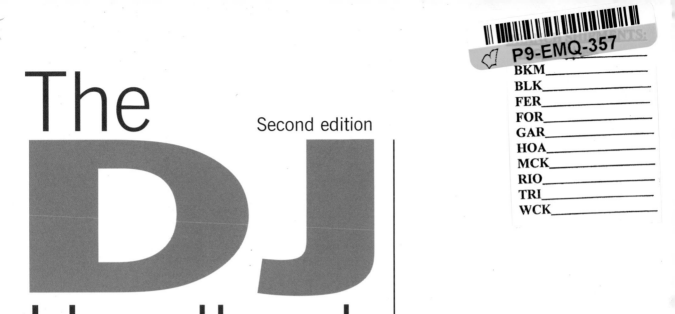

Charles Slaney

PC Publishing
Keeper's House
Merton
Thetford
Norfolk IP25 6QH
UK

Tel +44 (0)1953 889900
Fax +44 (0)1953 889901
email info@pc-publishing.com
website http://www.pc-publishing.com

First published 2006

© PC Publishing

ISBN 1 870775 99 6

British Library Cataloguing in Publication Data
A catalogue record for this book is available from the British Library

Cover design by Hilary Norman Design Ltd

Printed and bound in Great Britain by Biddles, Kings Lynn, Norfolk

Preface

'Djing. It's got to be about the music.'

When I wrote the preface for the first edition the phrase above was the first one that sprang to mind and it is still relevant. Certainly it was my love of soul music, which was the dance music of its time, that inspired me to become a DJ. And even though I say it myself, I ended up being quite a good DJ, or so I am told. I can't be that bad because 36 years after I first started I am still being sought out and getting paid work and enjoying it.

When I first started there was no 'DJ' equipment around, every rig looked like it had been made on Blue Peter. The turntables were little beige coloured Garrard things, there were no headphones, no cross faders or kill switches, sometimes not even volume controls, and some people have the nerve to call those the good old days. The DJ was a low life, the musicians hated you because they reckoned you were doing them out of work, you were not deemed to have any skill and the pay wasn't that good. Why bother? you might ask. Well when you are a shy seventeen year old, with no car and no money and they want you to work in the places you want to go to but can't afford, what would you say? If now, someone turned round to you and said fancy working as a DJ in Ibiza this summer would you say no? Thought not, you'd say yes first and then panic about the money and everything else later.

This book isn't a history lesson, although there's a bit of history in it, and it doesn't claim to be a technical manual, although there is a lot of technical stuff which should be useful, especially if you like life. Neither is it the sentimental ramblings of an old DJ. What I am trying to do here is give you insight and information which will help you become what you want to be.

It wasn't until I did my HND that I realised how much danger both I and my equipment had been in over the years and I don't want anyone to make the same mistakes I did. With that in mind you will find safety, both personal and otherwise, is an issue which I have tried to cover comprehensively.

So is it still about the music? Well I think so, I think that you, if you want to be a DJ, have got to love music, not necessarily be musical, but you have to know what sounds good and what doesn't sound good. Not just because it's in the charts, or just because MTV play it, but because it sounds good and it's good to dance to.

If you are a mobile DJ then perhaps music is secondary to your responsibility to entertain the crowd. You might have to play some suspect pop but it's all music, as long as they love it, that's all that counts and that's your buzz, the people having a good time.

My main hope for this book is that you will take away from it some practical assistance in moving towards your goal to be a DJ. I hope that some things will be made easier for you, that you will develop an understanding of the invisible processes at work and the skills required to make it in this business. If you do it right, it won't seem like a business, you'll be having too much fun to notice.

This second edition will explore the world of mixing in far greater depth and hopefully allay some of the mystery that surrounds what, broken down to its simplest components, is rhythm and beat matching.

DJ James Camm, who is one half of the recording artist Oliver James (with his studio partner, you've guessed it, Ollie), is donating a chapter detailing his progress and adventures starting as a DJ, then going into music production and promotion.

We will also take a look at some new gear on the market and take a look at live PA systems v passive ones (live means amps, speakers and crossovers in the same box, passive means you put it together like a jigsaw) for the mobile DJ and we take a deeper look at Hazard Analysis, which I call common sense, but we will look in greater detail and what is expected of you in this regard.

About the author

Charles Slaney has been involved with the DJ and club business since 1969. In that time he has been involved in many aspects of the industry and through all of the technical innovations that have brought Djing into the 21st century.

He still works as a club and mobile DJ, and has designed and installed Disco/PA systems from Oxford to Grangemouth. In the seventies he managed the Manchester branch of DJ Equipment retailer Roger Squires before going freelance as an installer in the eighties. Now, as well as Djing and writing, he acts as an informal tutor and trouble shooter, passing on his knowledge and experience to a range of DJs who are working in both the club and mobile DJ business.

In 1998 he completed an HND in Professional Sound and Video Technology at Salford University, followed by an Honours Degree in Film & TV Studies at The University of Wales, and is currently completing an MA in Screenwriting Fiction at Leeds Metropolitan University, all as a mature student.

Thanks for their invaluable assistance and continued support to:

Mark Stanton Hughes (real name),
'Derbs' Erfyl Lloyd Davies,
'Marky Mark' Odam,
James Camm AKA Oliver James
Randy Billingham 'Mr.B's Disco'
(All DJ's)
My wife Suzie, my kids. Liza and Ricky Morris (all critics)
Rob Platt for putting me on to M Audio, and ringing me up to play kicking tunes down the phone
Photos: David Andrew, Charles Slaney, James Camm.

Contents

What is a DJ?

A DJ or Disc Jockey is basically a person who plays recordings of musical works (which have been made by other artists) to audiences, who listen and/or dance. DJs were once considered to be the lowest form of human life in the entertainment and media industry. But now, in the fickle world of show business, those who were once the lowest in status are now amongst the most highly paid and respected.

Radio DJs began as presenters, and some of these well known individuals wouldn't even recognize a turntable. The music they played was chosen for them, the words they said were read from a script, they were, to all intents and purposes, continuity announcers. In the 1960s, in the UK, the pirate radio stations and Radio Luxembourg were exciting because they played records, especially black music, which the establishment radio (BBC) didn't play.

Even in 1967, with the birth of Radio 1, things didn't change much. There were just different people reading the scripts, written by the last generation who were trying to control the emerging generation. The DJs who were to make a difference were in the clubs. It would take another 30 years before this was recognized by the generation 'brought up' in those clubs.

Recently I heard that DJing is something 'you just do or learn as you go along', which I find to be a strange idea. Given today's environment, with the sophistication of equipment, techniques and the related safety issues, it would seem to me that teaching is essential for safe and happy progress.

Many people are referred to as being DJs. For the purposes of this book a DJ is, for the most part, a person who plays CDs/records to an audience. The audience can be seen by the DJ and interacts with him/her. Some material on hospital-type in-house 'radio' systems will be included but we are mainly concentrating on working DJs doing live shows. I'm narrowing the definition to exclude TV presenters, radio presenters and groups of otherwise indefinable celebrities who are labelled as DJs. The DJ is the person who will, during the course of the event, programme and play the music, make the announcements, incite and control the audience as required, get them up to dance, sit them down, introduce the cake, etc.

Some of these DJs will be on the cutting edge of musical culture, most won't, but every one of them has the capability and opportunity to impose his/her tastes on the audience, attract a unique following and exert influence over individuals' lives, whilst earning an income. It sounds pretty far-reaching and it is.

To those of you who merely think of DJs and their equipment as nothing special, here's a thought for you. A modern product that has entertained millions of

DJs were once considered to be the lowest form of human life in the entertainment and media industry. But now, in the fickle world of show business, those who were once the lowest in status are now amongst the most highly paid and respected.

Figure 1.01
The Technics SL 1200 – a design classic.

people, in spite of now being 20 years 'out of date', is the Technics SL1200 turntable. It is a DJ's tool and as such, whether people realize it or not, at some time or another they will have listened to music that has been played on it. Like the Aga and the Swiss Army Knife, it is a design classic, and in a world of computers, CDs, MDs and Mp3s, it is an antique. In the USA, it has been reported that in the 21st century, individuals wanting to go into the music business buy a turntable rather than a guitar.

The 'master of the dance' has always been a very important figure in human society because dancing is a fundamental activity. The modern DJ is the master of modern dance. In our sophistication, we forget that our need for rhythm and music is accompanied by our need for someone to control and deliver it. So the DJ has emerged from being the musician's sworn enemy and extra glass collector at the end of the night to become a pivotal person within the room.

Before this goes to your head and you start strutting, remember that just because the DJ is important, it doesn't mean that he/she is irreplaceable; and with this bestowed responsibility comes the added duty of care to those in the DJ's temporary charge. As well as being master of ceremonies, the DJ may have to be a van driver, loader and shifter and electrical, plus acoustic, engineer. There are many skills involved with what at first glance may seem to be a simple and glamorous job.

In the beginning

Where did it begin? Well DJs have been around since someone decided it would be a good idea to play a new invention called a 'recording', on another fairly new invention, the phonograph, on a new discovery called the radio. According to 'Last Night a DJ Saved My Life; The History of the Disc Jockey' by Bill Brewster and Frank Broughton, the first record was played on the airwaves in 1906.

The term 'disc jockey' originated in America and was used to describe the guy who played the records, or at least introduced them. In the 1950s, the 'DJs' as they were then known, became more influential. After all, to be a DJ you just needed a big mouth and a little personality, which suggested you were probably closer to reality than most and that you were more able to communicate with a popular audience. Maybe the most famous American DJ was Alan Freed. He was credited with calling rhythm and blues by the name 'Rock n' Roll', therefore creating the 'genre'; he is also credited with staging the first 'rock' concert. It was Alan Freed who introduced us to contemporary black music, which has revolutionized all music that followed. For him, it was definitely about the music.

The Alan Freed type of DJ was a compere. He introduced live acts at shows and jamborees and played records on a radio station. It was another development, widely credited to a Yorkshireman called Jimmy Savile, that ensured DJs would appear on their own, in the form as we now know them, in clubs and as mobile DJs.

Sir Jimmy Savile OBE was Britain's, and probably the world's, first modern DJ. He ran dancehalls in Yorkshire and the Northwest of England, as well as being a wrestler and showman. It is Jimmy who is widely credited with creating the roles of the club and mobile DJ, as they are today. In the late 1940s and early 1950s, he cobbled two record players together and played his collection of 78rpm American swing records, loud, in dance halls. It didn't take Jimmy long to realize that this was cheaper than hiring a band to play live. And the records didn't need a break, didn't get drunk and he could play every popular song that was around. That was it, the DJ, as we know him was with us and has been ever since.

My first job was for a guy who was working at Jimmy Savile's Top Twenty Club at Belle Vue in Manchester, who needed his other job, on the same night, covered. Apparently he had been let down by his regular stand in, so a mutual acquaintance gave him my address (no-one had telephones in 1969). He came to see me and said 'I hear you're a bit of a DJ'. Of course I wasn't, I was a spotty teenager who had only ever played a few records on a Dansette at the local youth club for his mates, but I answered 'Yeah'. Half an hour later I rolled up to a room above a pub in Reddish near Stockport, with the promise of earning ten shillings a night (that's 50p in today's money) and in a sheer panic.

When I looked back for inspiration to help write this book, I realized that I was fortunate to see and work alongside some really influential DJs who shaped much of what we currently take for granted in the 'dance' music scene. I now pay my respects to Brian 'Do The 45' Philips (The Twisted Wheel), Colin Curtis (The Torch and Rafters) and the legendary John Grant (Rafters), for being men ahead of their time and leading where the rest of us were to follow.

You will hear a lot of older people decry the modern scene, saying 'they don't make records like they used to'. Thankfully they don't, but personally (and I know the guys named above will agree with me), I believe some of the new stuff is absolutely superb, different from, but no less good than, anything we've ever heard. The equipment available to work with is out of this world, in comparison to 'the good old days'. So enjoy it, I do, and I'm one of those older people.

There are brilliant, talented musicians out there and they need someone to showcase their music. Some individuals can play five or even ten different instruments, but the DJ can play them all. Dancing is an activity that is as important to the human species as breathing and eating; the DJ filters and chooses the music used for much of this dancing. The role has a history that is longer and deeper than a glance at the latest technology would suggest. This equipment enables the DJ to exist as a DJ in his current form. The music the DJ plays has been and will continue to be an extremely important social and cultural influence.

Now you know what you are getting yourself into.

2 Basics of DJing

As we meander around the vagaries of being a DJ, let's get some DJ basics onto paper. Here are some essentials you will need to have, know or do. Some apply more to club life than mobile gigs, but all are relevant:

- Have a driving licence. Keep it clean. (You can't get around without one.)
- Have a strong aversion to drugs and alcohol. (You can't work if you're drunk or stoned, if you are inclined to be either or both, give them up or don't be a DJ.)
- Know how to dance. I know a few DJs who can't dance a step but really, how can you say this is a banging dance tune if it doesn't move you.
- Have determination and perseverance; your attempts to become a DJ, especially a club DJ, will appear to be thwarted at every turn.
- Do hang around where it's at in your locality, become a 'face', get to know managers and security, they get you into places.
- If you are to be a club DJ, do try to get onto mailing lists, it will save you a fortune and keep you up to date.
- Know your subject. There are so many sub-groups or genres that I wouldn't even attempt to name them here. Whichever is yours, know it inside out and back to front.
- Never slag anybody off. If you are ever asked your opinion about another DJ, make sure that what comes out of your mouth is praise. If you can't praise them don't say anything, slagging people off only makes you look bad.
- Keep all your equipment, or the equipment you use, clean, tidy and in good working order, all the time.
- Never promise what you can't deliver and always keep your word.

In the clubs, the people who pay you are not, as you may think, the customers, it is the management. It's they who decide whom to use, how often and for how much. Believe me when I tell you the polite, punctual, reliable, steady DJ will always get more work than the wayward, talented, volatile, moody, sometimes genius, 'may not turn up', DJ. If you can work well as part of the team and get yourself a bit of respect from the security and management, you will get the work. Managers always check you out before they take you on and when they phone around, it's always other managers or security they talk to, never customers.

So that's your 'hit list' if you like, things that will increase your chances of gainful employment, but of course it's never just that easy. There is a whole parallel process that you have to go through at the same time. Some of it is involved with the list above, some of it will be mentioned here and covered in other chapters. Some things will apply to MC type or mobile DJs that don't apply to hard house mixers and so on. You will have to pick the bones out of it all to see what is relevant for you.

For example, you all need to know about equipment. Club DJs need to know how to balance the arm of a turntable, set the anti skate, how to fit a cartridge. You all need to know how to set the gain structure of the mixer, all mixers are different but gain structure is always the same. You all need to know the component parts of mixers from the operational point of view. Some of you will need to know more about EQ, room reverberation and delays, CD player capabilities, MiniDiscs™ and so on.

Irrespective of where you want to end up, I think learning to use a microphone is a must. Obviously, the mobile DJ doing weddings and parties and functions is going to use the mic more than a hard house mixer, but really that's no excuse for not learning to use a mic.

Mix DJs need to be able to count (am I stating the obvious?) – beats to the bar and bars in an instrumental break, very hard to master. Counting beats is easy but knowing where a bar starts and which beat to use to drop or slide your mix in on, is not as obvious as you might think. Hopefully the expanded chapter on Mixing and how it's done will not only inform you about the mechanical process, but will go someway into explaining the 'musical' or 'performance' side, essential to modern DJing.

Tip

Irrespective of where you want to end up, I think learning to use a microphone is a must.

General equipment

You need to have your own headphones and microphone; they are yours, you don't lend them, leave them or lose them. Whichever microphone you choose, make sure it has an on/off switch. Why? Well you are not a rock singer, with an engineer controlling your levels and a noise gate on your line. An open microphone adds noise into the system, so while a Shure SM58 might look cool when you put it down, it's still switched on. Rest it on a flat surface and it's going to start humming, put it in a stand and it's going to send room noise through your system. You don't want to be switching the mic on at the mixer or turning the volume control up and down every time you use it. You want to be able to switch it off, without it clicking. This type of microphone whilst 'resting' during a gig is not adding noise into the system or taking up headroom.

Headphones have got to be user friendly. I'm now on Beyer DT250's, but there are a plethora of 'cans' which are just as good, so choose yours, put them in your case and that's what you use.

Other stuff

Good personal hygiene is a must, don't be a stinker in the BO department, and stay away from the garlic and curries before working. You have to communicate at short range – you are in a loud environment – and the person you are close to will not appreciate bad breath or excited armpits.

An often ignored safety aspect, especially if you are working in a club, is securing your own supply of drinking fluids. Some people think it's amusing to slip things into people's drinks; I have seen this happen and have had to phone for an ambulance.

Dress is an important part of being a DJ. Dress appropriately for the occasion; and don't wear a heavy wool suit for Saturday night in a sweat pit if something light would be more comfortable. If you are a mobile DJ, a change of clothes is a good idea. Set up and strike in scruffs, work in best; it not only looks professional but you feel better and give a good impression to your next potential client who is in that crowd.

Basic toolkit for the mobile DJ

Everything but the kitchen sink. Spare leads, at least two of everything in the leads department. Adapters for converting XLR to jack, phono to jack, jack to phono, everything to everything. Spare fuses for every item of equipment and every mains fuse rating. You will need a multimeter and if the finances run to it, at least one spare amplifier. Screwdrivers and long nose pliers are handy too. An invaluable aid is a little freestanding clamp for holding things while you solder. A soldering iron or gun and solder, a torch and a couple of rolls of gaffa tape. This lot lives in a little toolbox and never leaves your van.

Basic toolkit for the club DJ

This is quite a difficult one, since in theory everything should be in the club. It would be a good idea to carry spare cartridges if you use vinyl, plus some small screwdrivers and long nose pliers. A headband torch is handy, clubs are always dark even in the middle of the day.

The business of DJing

3

Make no mistake, DJing is a business, a big business. We have already covered some of this in Chapter 2 and later on is other information concerning the business of being a DJ. In this chapter, there are some specifics that may assist you, assuming of course that you want to get paid for what you do and that you want to get work in the first place.

The schmooze

Schmoozing is a word that you hear a lot in hospitality and media circles. It's used to describe the gentle manipulation of those people who may help in forwarding your prospects and maintaining or increasing your profile. For example, an actor looking for work will schmooze people who can get him/her work – casting directors, agents, directors etc. Similarly, you as a DJ will schmooze the people who can get you work – agents, club managers, headline DJs. Never think you are too important to schmooze because you never will be. There is no excuse either for being distant, sullen or discourteous; for not saying please and thank you and for not inquiring if everything was to your employer's satisfaction, your employer being the person who pays you.

First time in a new club, first spot, don't walk in like you are a superstar because you're not. Introduce yourself to security, to the manager, to the bar staff, to the cleaner, because you are now part of that team. You are no more important than any other member of that team, try to be and you won't be in that team long. Respect the people around you if you want to gain their respect.

Club people are a strange bunch, they tend to congregate and talk to each other. Someone will see you somewhere and ask someone else, 'who's that?' and be told 'that is Dirk/Dirkess, one of our DJs'. Your name is now in the circle. If you hadn't taken the time to let that person find out your name, the answer to the question would be a shrug, your name is not in the circle.

Schmoozing doesn't mean creeping or sucking up to people, it means making people feel warm and tingly about you, yeah even the 7ft animal on the door with arms like an anaconda, can feel warm and tingly about you. All you have to be is polite, pleasant and part of the team – you will get served more quickly at the bar too.

Similarly, for the mobile DJ the procedure is much the same. Don't turn up at the venue and say 'I'm the DJ, can you get that car moved so I can get my van 4ft closer'. If you have never worked at a place before you should, if at all possible,

Tip

First time in a new club, first spot, don't walk in like you are a superstar because you're not. Introduce yourself to security, to the manager, to the bar staff, to the cleaner, because you are now part of that team.

make a prior recce of it. Visit the venue, ask for the manager or owner, introduce yourself and explain that you have been contracted to provide a mobile DJ service on a given date. Could they please show you where you will be working, where is it best to bring in your gear, where would they like you to leave your van, what time is best for you to set up, what time the buffet will be served, what time you are expected to finish, and are there any dos or don'ts?

During your enquiry, the management will make you aware of any potential pitfalls or problems that you may come across. You will view the room acoustically, find out where the electricity supply is and behave in a professional manner. More importantly you will be able to do a hazard analysis, involving yourself unloading, moving in and setting up, and potential problems that might affect the public in doing that, and in your subsequent 'performance'. Don't arrive at a busy reception, demanding time and attention from the management when they can least afford to give it. The result is that when you leave your card with the manager, an enquiry that comes in for someone to provide a mobile DJ may be passed on to you, because at least you took the trouble to do it right.

So there you have a pocket guide to schmoozing, some people are very good at it and make it into an art form, people like politicians. The rest of us struggle, but the key is manners. It doesn't matter what anyone else around you is doing or saying if your own behaviour is beyond reproach. At the end of the night, thank the management for having you there and say goodnight. It's only manners but it's worth more than you think.

The brief

As a DJ you will be asked to do lots of different things, most of them will involve your impeccable taste in music and playing tunes of one description or another. It is however very important that you establish exactly what it is that is required of you. I have done in-house radio, wet T shirt competitions, disco dancing championships, car launches, strippers, and more than a few four-hour mixes.

The worst thing I tried to do (and I failed miserably), was the fill commentary before the start of a yacht race. I was coerced into the job and I was totally out of my depth, so to speak. I didn't actually know what was required and when push came to shove, I couldn't do it anyway. I had no idea about nautical terms, yachting or yacht racing. I thought all that was needed was background music and some witticisms about seagulls. Needless to say, my reputation was somewhat compromised because of a lack of information, which was totally my fault. I should have found out exactly what was required of me, before glibly agreeing to something that I didn't have the expertise to do.

As a result, now, before I take anything on, I make absolutely sure of what it is I am expected to do, without being pedantic or obstructive. Then when I get there, I do what has been agreed. Be warned, if you do not find out exactly what is required of you, you will at some stage come a cropper. It is so important if you are to do your job well and if a good time is to be had by all, that you are in possession of all the facts before you begin. If you aren't, you will find yourself turning up at what someone else thinks is a heavy metal thrash night, but what you think is a wedding party.

Getting paid

Getting paid for what you do is a very important part of this job, it is the life-blood of any business, big or small. It doesn't matter how talented you are, how good the product is, what good value is being given, if you don't get paid, you will fail. Every business will fail if it is not paid for the work it does or the product it supplies.

Things are a lot better in the club business than they used to be. Not so long ago club personnel used to behave as if they were doing DJs a favour by letting them work there. This is still the case in a couple of places, so don't go there. And warn everyone else. If you must, use these places for practice then leave. That club will have to wise up, or its customer base will vanish to where the good jocks are – good jocks are the ones being paid.

Even so, every so often you will get cheated, in that case it's your job to make sure they don't do it to you twice and hope they think again before they do it to anyone else. Many years ago, I turned up at a club for a theme night I had done a couple of times before. The manager had changed since I last worked there but I knew his replacement and he knew my terms. At the end of the evening he short-changed me. I have been asked to work there since but I have not done so. You must not allow people to get away with not paying you what has been agreed, unless of course there are very extenuating circumstances (there were not in this case).

On the mobile DJ scene, it can be even worse. You will be expected to load your van full of £5000 worth of equipment, drive to the venue, struggle up the fire escape in the rain, set it all up and work for four hours entertaining everybody; then take it all down, pack it away and drive home and be thankful for getting £50. No, I don't think so.

Part of this subject, Getting paid, is covered in the previous section – 'The brief', but the process of getting paid begins at the very start. You negotiate your price based on your level of expertise, the going rate for the area, the work you are expected to do and that's it. When you turn up, unless you have worked for the people before and have an ongoing relationship with them, the first thing you do, after you arrive and perhaps even before you set up, is to find the person who is responsible for paying you and relieve them of your agreed fee. They will be expecting this because you will have made this clear right at the beginning. If you are to be paid by cheque, you will ask to receive it no later than 10 days before the gig. You may or may not require a deposit, that is a matter for you.

Why? Well, imagine the scenario: it's a wedding reception, 300 guests, it starts at eight and finishes at midnight. Do you really want to be wandering around at 12:30 a.m. trying to find someone sober enough to tell you who has got your money? No. What if, after you have finished, they decide you were crap and now they don't want to pay you, what do you bargain with? No, the fee is better off in your pocket before you start.

The attitude towards payment also may vary regionally. I live in mid Wales and most of my work comes in via a good friend of mine whom I introduced to the business 15 years ago. I do any jobs that he can't do himself. The fee, the venue and the job have all been agreed, but half the time, I will have to fight for the previously agreed payment, they don't know who's got the money, or I will be asked to give some discount, after all it's cash in my hand. Can you imagine what would

Tip

It doesn't matter how talented you are, how good the product is, what good value is being given, if you don't get paid, you will fail.

happen if I tried to get my money when I finished? No, get the payment before you start. I have to say, in the main you will find that people are as good as their word and you will have no problem, but why make a situation worse than it need be?

There are still some people who seem to think 'It's only the DJ' and appear to go out of their way to cause you grief. (This is another very good reason to master the microphone, he who holds the mic is in charge.) A DJ I know went to work at a wedding reception, arrived at the up-market venue he had worked many times before, he set everything up and went to find the person who was paying him. A man he had never met or spoken to approached him. The man said that he was too expensive, that they could have found someone cheaper, they had no intention of paying the amount that had been agreed and that he'd better sort himself out and come up with a reasonable figure if he expected to be paid at all. The DJ took his equipment down and went home. The exchange was longer and more heated than I have described, but it ended up with the DJ leaving, in spite of last minute offers to pay more than had originally been agreed. Can you imagine what would have happened if he had not bothered to try and get his payment until the function had finished? Also, he didn't get a deposit. He does now.

This might sound cynical and hard but it isn't; there are people out there who will willingly take advantage of you because you are 'only the DJ'. They couldn't care less how much your equipment costs or how hard you have to work. However, if you are clear and unambiguous during the brief, life is easier for you when you arrive at the gig. One of the things about being professional is getting paid.

> ## Info
>
> There are people out there who will willingly take advantage of you because you are 'only the DJ'. They couldn't care less how much your equipment costs or how hard you have to work.

Club DJ contract; mobile DJ confirmation letter and contract

My thanks to James Camm for letting me reproduce the short contract that he regularly uses (page 11). He also has a more detailed one. Whichever is chosen depends on the circumstances of the arrangement. His agent makes the deal, the booking fee acts as a deposit, covers the agent's fee and any contractual expenses. The contract is short and sweet and to the point and is clear as to what is required from both parties, which is what everybody wants.

You will notice an interesting point, that James specifies the equipment he needs at the front end, the equipment which he will operate, irrespective of whoever else is on at the venue. I spoke to him about this and he quite rightly said it's about consistency of operation. He knows what he can do with the equipment he has specified, so why spend an hour learning the foibles of a different mixer when you can just use one you already know? (Another interesting point is that in the contract the DJ is referred to as 'The Artist'.)

I have spoken to some mobile DJs who are totally against having any paperwork, they say that it scares people off; they may have a point. My own experience is that word of mouth is a most unreliable way to reach any agreement or pass on any important information that needs to be retained. If someone else's interpretation differs from yours, bad feeling can arise. Why risk it, when it is so much easier to avoid any doubt with a couple of sheets of A4 paper? The sample mobile letter I use for gigs is shown on page 13, and the confirmation I ask the client to return to me is shown on page 14. These serve me well and have certainly come in handy from time to time for clarification purposes.

A N OTHER
DJ performance Contract & Confirmation

Agreement on this day XXXXXX between XXXXXX representing A N Other
(hereinafter referred to as the 'The Artist') and XXXXXX
(Hereinafter referred to as the 'Employer'). The Employer hereby engages the artist, and the artist hereby agrees to perform the engagement hereinafter provided, upon all the terms and conditions herein set forth.

1 Employer. **XXXXXXX**

2 Venue. **XXXXXXXX**

3 Address. **XXXXXXXXX**

4 Date of performance. **XXXXXXXXX**

5 Hours of performance. **12-30am till 3am**

6 Fee: **XXXXX   +10% Booking fee.**

7 The DJ should appear on all promotional material as 'A N Other'

8 Payment terms: 100% booking fee in advanced, payable immediately upon signing this agreement.100% balance due on the night of performance in **CASH**. The booking fee will be non refundable, unless the engagement is cancelled by default of the artist.

9 The employer shall provide at its own cost a minimum of 2 Technics SL1210 turntables equipped with Stanton cartridges, 1 Pioneer DJM500 or DJM600 mixer, and two quality monitors pointing towards the DJ at ear level. The turntables must be mounted on a isolated secure unit to prevent feedback and vibration.

10 The employer agrees to ensure that there shall be no unauthorised filming or recording of any kind of the artist's performance. Furthermore, the employer agrees not to commit the artist to any personal appearances without prior agreement by the artist.

11 At the venue, the employer shall provide A N Other's rider which is as follows, 1x lockable dressing room, 24x bottles of cold Budweiser and up to 10 guest list places.

12 Artist obligations hereunder are subject to detention, or prevention by sickness, inability to perform, accident, means of transportation, acts of god, riot, sickness, strikes, labour difficulties, epidemics and acts or order of any public authority or any other cause similar or dissimilar, beyond the artist's control. In such events, the employer shall have the choice to either reschedule the performance with the artist at the earliest available date, or to receive a full refund deposit. (Excluding booking fee).

13 This agreement may not be changed, modified or altered without prior approval by an authorized representation of both employer and artist.

Signed (promoter)   Date

Signed (artist)   Date

Now these are not intended to be ultra legal documents but they are binding, although a solicitor would probably rip them apart (but only if you agreed a fee and then paid him). What these documents do is take away any ambiguity about the arrangement you have reached with your client and they do so well before the event. You fill in all the details. The client's job is to check them, sign at the bottom saying he has read and understood the terms and conditions and has kept a copy. Then he/she sends a signed copy back to you, with the deposit.

It is guaranteed that you could have many arguments over what it was perceived you would do, rather than what you agreed to do, if not for these pieces of paper. They remove all that grey area. What's more, it looks professional, instills confidence in the client, it gains you respect and it does away with any doubt. It takes five minutes to knock up on a PC, the cost is two stamps and two envelopes and already you are being recommended as being professional and efficient in your approach. If it's a wedding, the mother of the bride thinks you are marvellous, it's one less thing for her to worry about on the big day.

You could go on and get a 50-page contract to cover every angle, but that's not what it is about. It is about focusing your mind and your client's mind on exactly what it is that is going to happen, when, for how long and for how much. It also says, you can't just mess me about, we have an agreement.

A problem is, being a DJ is sort of a laid back social activity, very often bookings are made and taken on a casual basis and, dare I say it, a lot of your potential customers in the mobile business, are friends of friends. Well the surest way to lose a friend is not to be up front with them, or mislead them, so however casual the arrangement seems to be at the start, you make sure that you formalize it, in the long run everyone is better off.

Wanna be a great DJ?

What does it take to be a great DJ? Well, as I have said it's got to be about the music. A DJ can showcase great music from many different musicians and sources. The great DJs have been the innovators, those who brought new music to the masses. A really great DJ takes an obscure or little known genre and propels it to the forefront of popular culture. There are many musicians whose work would have remained unknown, had it not been sought out by the great DJs of the past and showcased on their behalf.

We are all now aware of the soul scene, started in rainy Manchester in the 1960s, which became known as Northern Soul, whose beat pattern is exactly the same as modern dance music, at around 135 bpm. Without the DJs who catapulted that music into mainstream consciousness, where would dance music be today? Similarly, during the evolution of the Jazz Funk idiom in the mid to late 1970s (those riffs are constantly sampled today, as the basis for modern dance music), the songs were pioneered by great DJs who went to notable lengths and expense to procure the product.

Many of these DJs had to fight against the cultural prejudices of middle class white society, enjoying the product of mainly black musicians. As a result of that prejudice, many black musicians who created great music in the 50s, 60s and 70s, lived in poverty and obscurity because the (white controlled) media would not allow

Sample Mobile Letter and Contract

Heading and Address

Client Name and Address

Date

Dear ....

Thank you for the booking to provide a mobile DJ service at your (wedding reception, party, anniversary) at the .... on the .... of................

I have enclosed for your attention confirmation of the service provided and the fee agreed. I have also enclosed a SAE for return of one copy of the confirmation signed as accepted by you, with your deposit. If between now and the date of the function you need to amend anything or require any further information please do not hesitate to contact me, my contact details are above.

I look forward to us having a great (evening, time) together.

Yours sincerely

Sample Confirmation

Heading and Address

Client Name _____

Address _____

_____

_____

Tel no _____

Music requirements _____

_____

_____

Tracks to be supplied by Client

_____

_____

_____

Type of party (birthday, wedding reception etc)

_____

Venue _____

Address _____

_____

_____

Tel no _____

Contact name _____

Function date _____ Time start _____

Time finish _____ Set up time _____

Special Instructions (if any) _____

_____

_____

_____

Service Provided:

To provide a mobile DJ service for a wedding reception/birthday party/engagement at the _____ on the ____ of _____ between the hours of ____ and ____ . The total fee that has been agreed between us for this service is £ _____

Signed _____ (DJ)

Dated _____

To be signed by the client

I have read and understood the terms and conditions and am enclosing payment in the sum of £ _____ as deposit, the balance to be payable in accordance with Clause **3**.

I have checked all the details which are correct/ I have modified. I have kept a copy of this confirmation for my own records.

Signed _____

Dated _____

Terms and Conditions

1 If the DJ has to withdraw from this booking for any reason at any time all money paid to that date will be refunded in full.

2 In the event of the Client cancelling this booking provided that there is 3 months or more to go to the date of the function the deposit shall be returned in full. If cancellation takes place less than 3 months before the function date the deposit will not be returned unless a substitute booking is taken, in which case the deposit will be returned in full. If there is less than 14 days to go before the function date and other bookings have been turned down and a substitute booking cannot be found then the balance of the fee will be due, unless there are agreed extenuating circumstances.

3 A deposit of £ ____ is due now with the balance of £ ____ being due in cash on the day of the function before the function begins. If that payment is to be made by any means other than cash then the due date for receipt of that payment is ten days before the function.

4 This service is provided at the request of the client and no liability will be accepted for any occurrence resulting from providing this service all such liability shall reside with the client. Any damage to any DJ equipment caused maliciously or accidentally during, or as a result of the function shall be deemed to be the responsibility of the client.

their talents to be showcased. This still goes on, there is music from all over the world which we have never heard in our society.

So being a DJ is not a waste of time or a soft option. Should you decide to take this mission, you have a choice as to how important you will be in the scheme of things. Learn the skills you need to do the job, but remember it's got to be about the music. Which track you play next, how long you can keep them up on the dance floor, how many people come to you at the end of your night and say that was really great, that's what makes a great music DJ.

The other type of great DJ is the showman DJ, the personality DJ. Here the music may become secondary to the person playing it, but you can bet that when he or she started, this wasn't the case. How do you become a great showman DJ? By being a great showman of course, by attracting attention to yourself and what you do and by being an expert schmoozer. All these things are important, as is the way you sound and come across. If you intend to try for radio you need a good voice and if it's TV and personal appearances you go for, clearly the way you look becomes a major issue.

This is an area where you either have 'it' or you don't. In addition to 'it', there is a lot of hard work and luck involved, much networking to be done and it is still very much a case of being the right person at the right time in the right place.

The DJ is no longer just a master of ceremonies, he is an artist in his own right. The great DJs of tomorrow will probably owe more to original performance as artistes than did the great DJs of yesteryear, who introduced us to class acts by other artists. It will not be so much about choice of the music but more about uniqueness of the whole product.

The future

James Camm's chapter (Chapter 11) is a practical example of a potential career path – there are several. I think that, given the available technology, the DJs themselves will take over the production of more and more of the music they use. This will not happen with the mobile DJs, playing to order at social events. But club DJs certainly, in their quest for uniqueness and exclusivity, will be programming their sets with more of their own stuff, produced in their home studios. After all, anyone with a computer and a little software can produce credible music, especially since modern dance music is particularly centred on rhythm and instrumental performances, rather than lyrics and songs.

We have already seen a first wave of this, as the DJ producers like Sanchez and Morales regularly produce popular mainstream chart records. As the technology becomes more affordable, more people will use it; what's the point of playing the same records as everyone else when you have the opportunity to be unique? As a result, apart from a few records that cross over (from the underground dance scene to the pop charts) and where some DJs are contracted to produce mainstream programming, the dance or club scene will revert to the same status it had in the soul clubs of the late 1960s and early 1970s. Now as then, the music will be new and exclusive, but today it will be originating from a different source.

CD Blanks cost pennies, music production software and sample libraries abound, and more DJs are moving away from vinyl. The DJ makes his music, plays it out and sells copies for £5 each. Another source hears the track and starts to play it, demand increases, the DJ goes to a mainstream production company and so on. More dance hits will come from the DJs than from the record industry.

Equipment – what you need and how to use it

Being a DJ involves developing skills in the operation of various forms of equipment, some mechanical, some electrical. You have to be dexterous, observant, your hearing needs to be good and you need to be able to do all these things in a hostile environment. So it would seem to make good sense to profile the equipment about which you are likely to need an operating knowledge.

Chapter 5, Sound basics, will cover in greater depth what you need to know about technical aspects of controls you will operate. Here, we shall concentrate on the types and some makes of equipment you'll encounter. Before continuing, it must be stressed again that this book is not a technical manual, if you really want to know the ins and outs of any of the pieces of equipment overviewed here, there are other publications which cover the subjects in more depth. We are looking at the operating aspects and usage, rather than the technical nitty gritty.

For the rest of this section, we are going to split things into two groups, firstly looking at the equipment you would find in a dance club environment, then at what you would find in a mobile DJ's environment. That's not saying the dance clubs don't also promote 'mobile' events, like festivals etc., but the equipment they use for these is seemingly the same as for a fixed location, whereas a mobile DJ will use a different setup altogether. Before this, however, we will look at items that are commonly used in both branches of the sport.

Microphones

Whichever DJ you are, club or mobile, you will need a microphone. As stated elsewhere, the recommendation is that you have one with a switch. A low impedance microphone should be fine for most mixers you will use. Some microphones are available in dual impedance versions and can work with either high or low impedance inputs. You don't need one with particular characteristics to suit speech, with the exception of perhaps some bass roll off to negate handling noise, and a pickup pattern which cuts down the possibility of feedback. The figures overleaf show the frequency response graph and polar pattern (pickup pattern) of a Shure SM48S.

As can be seen the bass response rolls off from about 150 Hz down which means that handling noise is minimized and the polar pattern is unidirectional, cardioid and uniform around the axis which helps reduce feedback in a closed room.

My preferences are for Shure Unispheres or Unidynes, discontinued now, but various models of both are available on eBay from time to time. But I also have a

Frequency response graph of a Shure SM48S.

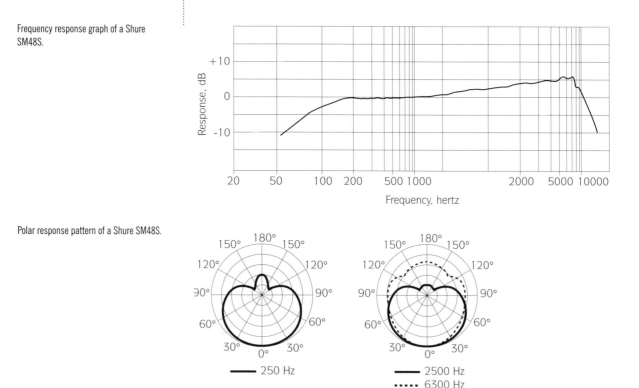

Polar response pattern of a Shure SM48S.

—— 250 Hz

—— 2500 Hz
····· 6300 Hz

Beyer M300 (with a switch of course), and with them, I carry several spare leads terminating in both XLR's and jack's. Whichever make or model you choose make sure it has an on off switch that doesn't click.

At this stage don't start thinking, uh oh cardioid, unidrectional? What does this all mean? You don't need to know, unless your intention is to start micing up orchestras in which case different instruments and mic placements require different characteristics. All you are looking for is a mic that won't make a noise on its own, that you can switch off when you put it down, and that you can speak into and it will reproduce your voice clearly without picking up the rest of the room.

For whatever reason you may prefer to use a Beyer, AKG, Behringer, Shure or another brand. Whatever your choice your preference should be based on practicality and price. The big tip is get one with a switch. You may prefer a radio mic, now you can convert your favourite wired mic into wireless using an AKG SO40, a transmitter/receiver device that fits an XLR duberry thing on the bottom of a normal mic which sends the generated radio signal to a receiver plugged into your mixer's mic input. Or if you want to keep both hands free for mixing, try a headset mic, available from Beyer, Shure and many others.

The AKG SO 40 transmitter and SR 40 receiver.

Basic microphone technique

How difficult can it be to use a microphone? All you do is switch it on and talk into it. Well actually it can be quite hard. The thing that is quite strange is that the voice coming out of the speakers doesn't sound like you because when you listen to yourself talk normally you hear the majority of the sound you are making inside your head, not through your own ears. When you use a mic, you only hear what comes out of the speakers, you don't recognise yourself. Add that to what you hear back from the room, which may have a little delay on it, and that really can throw you. A bit like waiting for your echo to die down before you speak again.

Once you have recovered from the shock of thinking you had a deep sexy voice when in fact you sound like Tiny Tim, you will also notice that any slight accent or intonation you have seems to be exaggerated. Well, your voice and its components have, along with everything else, been amplified, so that mild Geordie accent becomes stronger, the more amplification it's given; which might explain why a lot of media people who earn a living using microphones seem to be accent-less. I have a slight lisp, except when I'm using a mic, when I sound like a drunken Celt trying to say 'she sells sea shells on the sea shore'. It's a nightmare – but here are a few tricks and tips to help you through.

Firstly, resist the temptation to panic and speak as fast as you can. Suffer the pain and embarrassment of listening to your words, *speak slowly*. If you can't understand what is coming out of the speakers, neither can anyone else. As a general rule of thumb, adding bass to the mic channel does not make your voice sound deep and sexy, it makes you sound muffled and bumbling. Clean the mic channel up so your voice is crisp and clear; make sure the level is up to at least the same as the music channels.

The positioning of the mic is crucial. For live work, it should stay just underneath your bottom lip on your chin, when you turn your head remember to move your mic at the same time. Never cup the mic too closely under the windshield, or cover the windshield, it will feed back and make horrible noises. Never shout into a microphone, the microphone shouts for you, if you need to be louder, turn up the mic volume.

Have you ever wondered why people who test a mic say 'one, two' and never quite reach three? Well 'one' is for bass, 'two' is for treble. If you say 'one' slowly, opening your mouth wide and 'two' with your lips pursed on the first syllable, all will become obvious. I tend to add a 'tssst tssst' to my mic test, just to check how my lisp is going to sound. Learning to use a mic can be quite a trial but it doesn't matter how well you mix, you are never going to be in the top echelon unless you can conquer your fear of the mic. Make it your friend, it is an invaluable tool.

Headphones

Similarly, whichever type of DJ you are, you will also need headphones, commonly known as 'cans', to enable you to cue your records up and/or mix. Perhaps even more so than with microphones, this is a piece of equipment where personal preferences are important. Some people like to use closed cans that cover the ears completely, so all that can be heard is what's in the can. Some prefer the semi closed type, here, what's in the can is mixed with what's in the room. Some people will have one can over one ear and the room completely open in the other. Beyer DT100s, a closed type, were until a few years ago, the standard monitor headphone in use in TV, radio and recording studios throughout the world. They are comfortable, reliable and repairable, the only observation to be made about them is that you need to pick the right ones to suit the types of mixers you will be using.

> **Tip**
>
> Once you have recovered from the shock of thinking you had a deep sexy voice when in fact you sound like Tiny Tim, you will also notice that any slight accent or intonation you have seems to be exaggerated.

> **Tip**
>
> While converters are very useful, beware using them on mic leads, always use the right lead for the job i.e. Mono Jack for a high impedance input, XLR for a balanced line low impedance input. You may mysteriously lose signal (volume and bass) otherwise.

Beyer DT 250s are the new industry standard headphones.

Beyer DT100s at work under the chin.

The DT100s are available in many different impedance configurations, so if you get ones with too high an impedance for the mixer headphone socket, you may not get enough volume out of them in a loud environment, ideally they should be 100 ohms or less for most DJ mixers.

There are many different quality brands of headphones, the DT100s stand out because they can be worn under the chin, they are easy on/easy off and in a four hour night they are always comfy.

A fairly new arrival on the market are the Beyer DT250's; unbelievable sound quality and room separation and at around £80 they come in cheaper than DT100's. What's more, they are black, so you don't look as though you're wearing a pair of woolly ear muffs.

The semi open cans, where there is no choice but to mix what's in the can with the room, can be misleading. The sound in the room is going to be coloured and delayed by the room and if the mix needs to be spot on, you may find that using 'room to can' mixing will give you a less than accurate result. If you need to hear what's in the room, use the closed type and slip an ear piece off as and when necessary.

Walkman types and in-ear headphones are not intended or recommended for professional monitor purposes for DJs.

Turntables

Once upon a time there was only one turntable, the Technics SL1200 MkII. It is rumoured that for some reason, Technics let a couple of their patents slip and now every turntable looks like it wants to be a Technics. If you look at the photos of the different brands you can't tell them apart. If imitation is the sincerest form of flattery, that tells you all you need to know about the Technics.

The original Technics SL 1200 MkII. Up to Mk3 now.

Whichever turntables are installed they will have the same basic functions, a start button, a pitch control (usually on a slider), a speed selector for 33 or 45 rpm and that's about it. Some may have an additional reverse control and other goodies but usually the above is enough. In addition, there will be an anti skate control, an arm height control and an arm balance counter weight. The stylus or needle is usually a diamond, one of the hardest substances known to man, which scrapes through a groove on a plastic disc (not the hardest substance known to man), to collect vibrations to convert into a sound signal. You know where this is leading, you will presumably be using this equipment to earn a living so you don't want a damaged or chipped stylus cutting extra grooves in your precious vinyl. Neither do you want a heavy stylus digging a hole through your vinyl, because the arm is balanced incorrectly, or the needle skipping happily across your discs because the anti skate is wrongly set up. So check it all before you put it on any of your precious vinyl. It takes 30 seconds to change a stylus, 30 seconds to balance an arm and 1.7 seconds to set the anti skate, so you will have used a full 62 seconds to service a turntable. How much would a new 12 inch single cost?

Stanton 500AL cartridge and stylus.

The better turntables in use are direct drive with a $^1/_4$ turn start time or less. They will probably have braking systems to stop the turntable, the cartridge type will be MM which means 'moving magnet' and they will probably use an Ortofon or Stanton cartridge and stylus.

The club will have either two or three turntables up and ready for use and they will always have spare styli and cartridges. These turntables aren't much good for 'mobiles', they are expensive and heavy and don't particularly like being banged around in the back of a van. But flight cases are available and they can be carted about, with care. If you do decide to move them about, make sure it is with the tone arm heads (cartridge and stylus) off

Stanton Groovemaster integrated cartridge, headshell and stylus.

and safely packed away, the tone arm locked down and check the balance and skate *every* time you set up. Belt drive budget turntables are available and they look very like their direct drive cousins, but they are not first choice if you are serious about improving your mixing ability.

Personal preference is involved with your choice of turntables. In the case of clubs, discounts, budgets and deals will be relevant. Technics were the originals but Vestax, Gemini, Numark, Stanton, KAM and Denon are all in there, with well specified Technics look-a-likes vying for the turntable business. Whichever you decide on, make sure it's direct drive, not belt drive and it has a high torque $^1/_4$ turn start and that it doesn't slow down when you are holding a record on the slip mat.

CD players

CD players that used to be there just for fill purposes only are becoming much more of a creative fixture in the club business. Whilst the audio specs of most CD players are similar (they have a much greater dynamic range, and are not half as noisy as turntables), the features and facilities that modern 'pro' CD players offer are far ranging, from the ability to play DVD's MP'3's and CDG's (Karaoke), memory cards with data, remembering loops, holding several different loops, FX etc, etc.

Many clubs that are still using turntables just nip out to 'Richer Sounds' every so often and buy any CD player that happens to be the manager's special offer that week. They know that the quality will be superb and because it's only there for filling purposes, it doesn't matter what features it hasn't got.

'Professional' CD players are to be found in radio stations but increasingly, MiniDisc™ and especially computer 'juke box' systems are taking over. However amongst Mobile DJ's, and creative Club DJ's, the CD player is a very important tool. It means that instead of lugging round heavy vinyl, the DJ can carry round more, of the much lighter, CD's.

There are a myriad superb, professional CD kits available on the market. Pioneer set the standard for everyone to follow back in the 90s, by virtue of the features incorporated in both their DJ series of CD players and their complementary 'best fit' DJM mixers. Just playing with a pair of DJ500s using the cross fader on a DJM500, to start and reset the loops which had been precisely cued in the middle of a track, displayed the true capability of these machines.

The Pioneers are superb tools but they are expensive. Pioneer, having set up a market sector, charges a premium for its product. Nowadays most of the 'quality'-manufacturers are up to speed so check out Denon, Numark, Gemini, American DJ and all the others, before plunging in.

Tip

Many clubs that are still using turntables just nip out to 'Richer Sounds' every so often and buy any CD player that happens to be the manager's special offer that week.

In the first edition of this book I said that vinyl will be finished soon, but it's still hanging on in there. CDs in general are great for mobile work, they are light, easy to install and give superb sound quality. If you were brought up on turntables, the top loaders seem to be instinctively easier to use. Most units will play CDRs, which means all your old vinyl can be archived to CD. Thus it will get a new lease of life and if you have a computer and a basic sound editing programme (see section on Software in Chapter 13), you can remix your favourite tracks the way you think they should be heard.

The DJ market supports all three types of CD player. There is the top loader, like the early Technics SL-P1200, or the Pioneer 500 series; the slot loader like the Pioneer CDJ100s, or the Pioneer CDJ1000; or the motorised tray loader, like most of the others use. Having tried all three types, my choice, starting with the best would be:

1 Top Loader;
2 Slot;
3 Motorised Tray.

Again, this is a matter of personal preference. Those who (like me) come from a vinyl background, seem to find the top loader easier to assimilate. The motorized trays can appear to be slow and there are doubts about their sturdiness. In a limited light situation the top loaders are just so easy to use. Equipment has to be solid enough to be taken for granted, this doesn't mean that it is abused, just that it needs to be able to withstand the rigours of use whilst in a working environment. For me, the motorized tray CD players don't seem to inspire confidence.

Some CD players are available as a kit with a mixer and of course they are available as a separate unit, either twin or single. The problem with CD players is that they are all as good as each other, regarding specification and sonic quality, so you have to look at additional features, ease of use and reliability before making your decision. Since the technical specifications of most CD players are so similar, what differentiates them from each other are the add-on features, like seamless looping, varispeed, master tempo, scratching, effects, digital out etc. These perhaps are the features to look for if you are the creative type.

The Numark DMX 01.

Some mobile DJ's are using laptops, and playing MP3's. Numark market an iPod™ mixer called the IDJ, which you plug two iPods into and play from there, the means of delivery are changing all the time. The club guys are adding to their turntable skills using Pioneer CDJ-800's and 1000's or the less expensive Numark CDX's. For mobile work the new kid on the block, from Pioneer replacing the Pioneer CDJ-100, is the CDJ-200, which plays MP3 discs as well. There are a myriad of comparable models but Pioneers, again, just may have the edge. But still don't take my word for it, check them all out. Things have moved on quite considerably, and equipment that was once the domain of the superstar road show is now surprisingly accessible to us all.

Clockwise from top left
CDJ-1000 Mk2, Numark IDJ, Pioneer
CDJ-200, Numark CDX.

If you really must push the boat out, check out the Pioneer DJV-X1, yes it plays DVD's, and with all the features that you find on the CD players.

Setting up a turntable

All turntables are slightly different, so you will need to consult the accompanying manual to ensure that you are following the correct procedure. In general, however, the principles that govern the setup of a turntable and tone arm are as follows:

- the turntables must be on a level surface free from vibration.
- the grounding lead, if there is one, must be secured to a grounding point; either to one specified on the mixer or connected to another piece of equipment or the frame, which is earthed.
- the counterweight should be positioned so that the turntable arm is balanced,

to hang stationary in mid air, the counterweight indicator should then be zeroed before any increase is added.

- the needle/stylus should be free from defects, not too badly worn and be at the correct angle to the turntable platter with a vinyl disc on it. There is usually a jig that comes with the turntable which ensures the needle is positioned correctly within the headshell, in relation to the platter, if using a cartridge in an adjustable headshell. In addition there may well be an adjustable height control for the tone arm assembly, which also contributes to the setting of the stylus angle to the platter.

- the anti skate control should be set so that when the needle is in a spiral groove, moving inwards on a spinning record, the centrifugal force encountered trying to throw it outwards is counteracted. Too much anti skate will cause the needle to skip towards the centre, too little and it will be thrown out of the groove and skip off the record. (Do not set the anti skate until after you have balanced the arm.)

That's about it, although it sounds complex, once the main setting up is done, actually changing a stylus and checking everything, resetting the balance and anti skate will take just over a minute. With the combined headshell cartridge stylus assemblies offered by Ortofon and Stanton, it is possible to change a cartridge headshell and stylus and reset everything in just over a minute.

All turntables require the same settings but just may have slightly different ways of achieving them. Vinyl is very expensive and, unlike CDs, the disc comes into direct contact with the mechanism used to extract and reproduce the analogue sound information coded within it. This means discs wear out, but they will wear out considerably more quickly if the turntable is set up incorrectly.

Setting up a CD player

Open the box, get it out, plug it in. The surface has to be fairly level and free from vibration, ideally the CD player should not be angled more than 15 degrees off the horizontal. That's it.

Club mixers

This is an area where real snobbery exists, so I'll continue without trying to influence the battle for supremacy. Let's say that a decent mixer will have a trim control on each input; anything else is a feature, the trim control is a must. As before, the rest is a matter of taste, style and kudos; some have rotary kills, some have kill switches, some have punch in/out kills (kills are quick-acting EQ controls). Most now have replaceable cross faders, long throw channel faders and three band EQs. Some come with EQ scene memories. Everybody is in this market, even mixer manufacturers of renown like Allen & Heath can be found building a DJ mixer, illustrating the demand for quality and the importance of this market.

Depending on the venue or usage, the mixer will usually have at least two RIAA equalized phono inputs for the turntables, possibly three or four, and a mic input or two. Sometimes, there may be additional line inputs for CDs or other devices, or a channel will have a selector switch to change between phono and line. There

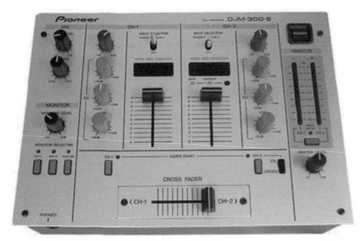

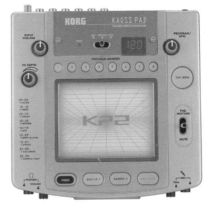

Clockwise from top left
Pioneer DJM300S, EFX 1000 Top, Korg KAOSS
Pad, DJM-1000.

will be a master out, a headphone out and there should be a VU meter per channel, or one that can be assigned to each channel, certainly for the music channels, and a cross fader. There will be a monitor selector switch that will give you PFL (pre-fader-listening) and perhaps there will be more mysterious goodies like effects units and samplers. The essentials are the first batch, with those you can take a signal into a mixer, check and set its input level, monitor it, mix it with what's playing out, kill the bass, bring the new track in over the old and tell everybody if there's a bomb scare.

In the mixer market, don't assume complexity equals quality, your mixer should be simple to operate and all the functions should be practical and useable.

Manufacturers are always looking for the latest idea to grab customers, be it better EQ more features or, more recently, the addition of internal FX or indeed independent FX units like Korg KAOSS Pads, or the Pioneer EFX-500 or 1000, of which James Camm is a fan. But don't take anyone's word for it, check what's out there, it changes literally every day.

Mixer manufacturers include Pioneer, Ecler, Rane, Denon, Behringer, Allen & Heath, Stanton, Technics, Gemini, Vestax, Numark, KAM, Korg, Roland and – a blast from the past – the original separate DJ mixer manufacturer Citronic, along with a few others. You will notice that for some reason a lot of mixer manufacturers still prefer black as a finish colour, why is anybody's guess, lighter is better. After all it's going to be dark, so any help in the area of small buttons and knobs is welcome. Which is the best one? Who knows? All modern mixers are pretty good on specification. There are no apparent brand weaknesses, it's a matter of choice, some have notably more pedigree than others do and there is a vast range. Obviously, you need to know what you will be doing with it, but most of the time four to six line/RIAA inputs and two mic inputs are all that will be needed.

Mobile mixers

If you are going to be a mobile DJ, you would do well to consider an all-in-one solution, where the mixers and CD players come as a package. Your gigs have to recoup the cost of the kit, so choose it accordingly. At the top end of the market are the slot loading Pioneers, the CDJ-800 and 1000 Mk2 with a DJM 500 or 600, or the DJM 300 (S is Recommended) and CDJ-200's for those with thinner wallets, who need to have a name in their case. There are also some really attractive budget deals, from Numark, Gemini, American DJ and the like. Remember the sound quality of all CD's is virtually identical, just less features on budget models. It really is down to size of your wallet and, of course, how much the kit will earn you.

The DJM 300S, in particular, is a cracking little mixer (the EQ, like all Pioneers, is a little clinical) suitable for all

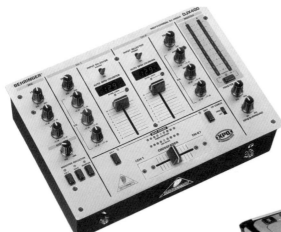

Behringer DJX400 and the Numark DJ in a box Fusion 111.

usages (club, mobile or home, scratching, synch starting CD's, whatever) simple to operate but comprehensively featured. However if anybody from Pioneer reads this, it would benefit greatly from two or even three band EQ on the mic channel, and XLR master outputs, like its big brothers. Behringer do a virtual copy the DJX-400, a lot cheaper, but without the remote start facility.

Home use mixers

If your intention is to buy a practice kit just for home use and you want to play vinyl, then you really don't need eight channels and effects and all that stuff, keep it as simple as you can. To practise mixing, you will need a couple of direct drive turntables into a two channel mixer, with channel trim controls and channel monitoring, a mixer starting price is around £80. That is all you will need and the principle will always be the same wherever you go from there. The temptation is to save money and buy the belt drive turntables, after all it's only for practice. Well, that's like practising for a Grand Prix in a Ford Fiesta. Nothing wrong with a Ford Fiesta, a good car, does its job perfectly well, but its job is not Grand Prix racing.

Other equipment — mobile DJ

Nine times out of ten, the only area a club DJ will have access to and influence over are the players and mixer. Everything else, crossovers, graphics, amps, speakers etc. will be dealt with by the house engineer(s). You mobile DJs however, well it's a different story.

We are assuming that, having got this far, you have your mic, headphones, CD players and mixer. Is there more? Well of course there is:

• Graphic equalizers
• Crossovers
• Amplifiers
• Speakers

All the above items are important, your CDs will sound great only if the rest of your kit is up to scratch. Speakers are like tyres on a car, it doesn't matter how expensive the car is, there are only four bits that ever touch the road. With speakers it doesn't matter how expensive the kit is, the only bit you ever *hear* are the speakers. The quality of the signal from your CD players and mixer is going to be excellent because you will have read and understood the technical section on Gain Structure (see Chapter 5). Now we need to get that excellent signal into the ears of your paying customers.

The basic equipment for a mobile DJ will be, in reverse order, speakers, an amplifier (active crossover) and a graphic equalizer, after the signal has left the mixer. The crossover, which in effect separates the high and low frequencies, will usually be a passive one which is built into the speaker cabinet, into which there will be installed a bass driver (woofer), a mid range speaker and a horn (a full range cabinet). The amplifier will be the correct rating for the speakers and the graphic equalizer will shape the sound that travels into the amplifier and then moves into the speakers.

Graphic equalizers

The graphic equalizer should be at least 2x15 band, with at least a 6–12dB attenuation per band and possibly a high pass filter as well. Every room is different and this is what the graphic is for, to compensate for the room and make the signal output from the speakers equal to the signal to be heard, irrespective of the room or other influences. If you really want to be posh, there is an equalizer made by Behringer caller the Ultracurve 8024 (the subject of a little section on its own – page 34). This will automatically EQ your room for you. It is truly amazing and your sound will be better, without you having to do a degree in acoustics.

Compressors

Compressors are adaptable to many different creative uses in recording music. For our purpose, as DJ's, we use them, mostly, to limit the signal levels going to the amplifiers from the preceding signal chain.

If you overdrive an amp constantly, at the least you will get distortion, you will certainly heat the amp up, as it tries to cope with an excessive signal levels. As you are working and you get used to the sound level, the tendency is to tweak it up, as the night progresses. Invariably the tweaking is done on the master output on the mixer, rather than bending down and turning up the amp. (Especially for those DJ's who still insist on whacking the amps up full, and then using the mixer to control; master levels.)

The compressor allows you to preset the maximum level you allow through to the amplifier. Especially useful as microphone use generates higher peak levels than continuous music does, so the resultant peaks are squashed into the allowable preset level.

Basically the compressor acts as a non-intrusive (set correctly) signal limiter, designed to protect your equipment from misuse and maintain sound quality. If you have a tendency to blow tweeters, and or speakers, a compressor in the signal chain could enhance your sound quality (especially in the area of bass) and save you money in the long run.

Crossovers

If you are running a big rig with more than one working amplifier and separate component speakers with bass bins, mid range cabinets and separate horns, you may well be using an active crossover as an additional component in your system. Active crossovers aren't cheap but they are good, you find that they are usually stereo 2/3 way and quoted at 18dB roll off per octave, which is good enough. The downside is that one amp per range is needed, so if you operate a three way active crossover

Behringer Ultradrive Pro DCX 2496, an electronic crossover, compressor, graphic equaliser, and sub harmonic processor in one unit.

you will need at least three amplifiers, bass, mid and top and some spares.

Most of the readers of this book will either be using full range speakers with built in passive crossovers, or will be working in clubs where the house engineers will look after the active crossovers.

Speaker control systems

The main piece of kit worth looking at here is the DBX DriveRack™ PA. What this unit does in essence is get rid of the two previous categories and, in total, at least four rack spaces of kit by combining (working backwards) a multi option electronic crossover, compressor, graphic equaliser, and sub harmonic processor in one unit. It's DBX so you know it's good quality. There are others available like Behringer's Ultradrive Pro DCX2496.

The DriveRack PA™ list of features is endless, with its own Real Time Analyser, and, with a bit of practice, you can get every room sounding good. The sub harmonic synthesiser operates in the same area as the Aphex (covered later) and the compressor section stops you popping speakers or at least overloading the input section of the amplifier. It is expensive at circa £400 but so are the individual four rack items it replaces, that said the price will come down and as always eBay is a good place to look. Consider buying an American one (around $400) and then plugging it into a converter plug to run 110V 60Hz from 220V 50Hz sockets.

Schematic of a three way tri amped system.

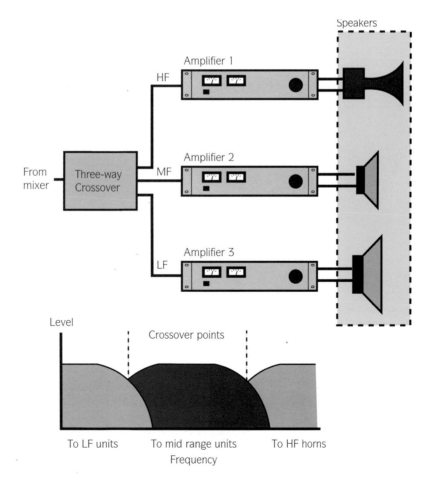

Amplifiers

Amplifiers are another area of snob value, certainly years ago when electrical components were distinctly less reliable than they are today, particular makes of amplifier were definitely better than others. Reading the spec for an amplifier can be baffling, but it has to be said that most of the modern 'named' amplifiers will give good service. If the speakers are 8 ohm and rated at 300 watts RMS, an amplifier that delivers 260 watts RMS into 8 ohms is going to be OK. If the speakers are 8 ohm and rated at 200 watts RMS, the same amplifier could destroy them, if run at the rated output. It is very important to ensure that speakers and amplifier are matched, if for some reason you have to run speakers that are rated at less than the amp's output, you had better make sure you never take that amp anywhere near flat out.

One overall guide to quality, is power. An 800 watt amp, running at half power will sound better than a 400 watt amp running flat out. It is the amp's ability to handle transients, which are peaks of voltage, without clipping and distorting that sets up the overall quality of the final sound. What makes for a crisp bass response is a high damping factor, though how high is the subject of great debate. The consensus is that a damping factor of 50 or above should be sufficient.

The quality of sound that the amplifier delivers to the speakers should not be coloured, or have any noise added to it, so the intrinsic quality generated by using a CD player (see Gain Structure, page 44) over a turntable should be retained through the mixer and the amplifier.

As the pros will tell you, there are only two or three brands that have unquestioning professional acceptance within the industry, one of these is Crown Amplifiers. In all professional setups, irrespective of what is used elsewhere, you should find Crown amplification. Now these amps aren't cheap, but they have a sonic purity, power and protection circuits that surpass all others. As always, in America they are cheaper than here, many of the models are variable power supply, which means they can be used worldwide, with no problem. The older ones, that aren't, are usually configured with jumpers to allow you, the user, to choose their voltage spec. I run two K2's bought from America, and courtesy of a no cost jumper replacement from the UK Crown Agent coupled with a change of fuse, I now have two 1250 watts (proper) per channel into 2 ohms, 800 watts into 4 ohms with a damping factor of over 3000. The clarity and power is incredible, the bass response is awesome. The K2 is especially useful for mobiles, where you are never sure about the power circuits you have to use, because of the low current draw compared to comparably rated amps. As I said, never as cheap as normal amps, even second hand, but far from normal amps. If you are truly serious about wanting to sound good, and don't want to worry about short circuits, open circuits and reliability, these are the only amps for you. Check out the Crown website for models and specs.

The Crown K2. If you are truly serious about wanting to sound good, these are the only amps for you.

Speakers

Most speaker cabinets for mobile disco use are self contained 'full range' cabinets, which means, technically at least they will reproduce frequencies between 40 Hz and 15 kHz reasonably well. The tendency for disco speakers is that they produce a lot of bass and top, with a mid section that sounds thin and tinny, that's the way it is.

If you are working on a big, high quality rig, the speakers will probably be of the component type. There will be a stack that looks after the bass and sub bass (probably in a mono configuration); there will be a stack that looks after the mid range and the low end of the high range (stereo); and there will be a stack (horns) that look after the tops or highs (stereo). It is more than likely that these will be controlled through an active rather than a passive crossover, and this will give a more naturalistic sound, should it be desired, than the full range disco speakers.

Active systems (amp in with the speakers) seem to gaining more fans amongst Mobile DJ's keen on cutting down the carrying and setting up time. A couple of mobile DJ's I know have invested in HK L.U.C.A.S active speaker systems, two small satellite speakers and a bass bin. Carry the lot in the back of a mini, they just run leads from their mixers to the bass bin, which also has the amps and crossovers in it, and then connect everything to that. It has to be said the sound quality is excellent and sufficient for most rooms. A lot of manufacturers, like FBT and Mackie offer active systems options, with improved electronic reliability they are well worth considering for Hi Fi sound at high volume levels, but they are not cheap.

Invariably when we talk about speakers we refer to speaker cabinets rather than components or speaker chassis. Since the last edition I have made a speaker 'chassis' discovery, amongst all the old favourites of JBL, Cerwin Vega, EV, RCF, Peavey etc., lurking very quietly, is a firm called Beyma, from Valencia in Spain. When one considers that speaker makers like Martin Audio use Beyma (and have you seen the price of their stuff?) and they equip a lot of European venues from Ibiza to Berlin, you know they must be good. As far as I can see they don't manufacture a speaker cabinet 'solution' just chassis for quality manufacturers like Martin. But Beyma's website gives you both speaker specs, and instructions for building cabinets to house them.

The Cerwin Vega V122 Mk1, a 12inch 2-way direct-radiating full range system.

If you want a light portable system and can't run to an HK or the like, the hot tip is a pair of Cerwin Vega V122 Mk1's up on stands with an 15inch or 18inch sub. Power the lot from one amp, but make sure it's a good amp, it will handle a crowd of 100-150 no problem.

There are a plethora of passive, and active, full range speakers on the market, remember the rules regarding RMS v peak (see below), and you can't go far wrong. It is important not to buy what the salesman needs to sell, you need to be sure that what you buy is right for your use, what makes a great PA system (Public Address System) may not make a good disco system, which needs a good round bass sound.

Impedance and resistance

You need to know how to work out the 'impedance' load you are putting on your amplifier when you connect your speakers. This will be covered in Chapter 5, Sound Basics also, but is included here because it is important and needs to be understood.

Amplifiers and speakers come with a rating, it's part of their 'specification'. Amplifiers may be something like 400 watts stereo into 4 ohms, speakers may be rated at 300 watts, 8 ohms. The first thing you need to grasp when discussing ohms, is that as far as amplifiers are concerned, less is more. In other words an amplifier that will go down to 2 ohms is better than an amp that will only go to 4 ohms.

Let's imagine that you are running a rig with an amplifier that delivers 400 watts stereo into 4 ohms (per side), but the speakers you are using are 300 watt (RMS), rated 8 ohms (per side). Do they match? Well a 400 watt amp driving flat out into 8 ohms will deliver about 60% – 70% of its rated 4 ohm output, say 240 watts into those speakers, so that will be within the speaker specification and within the amplifier specification. If you wanted to increase your output, you could add an extra speaker per side, rated again at 8 ohms. By doing this, in a *parallel circuit*,

Tip

When comparing specifications of speakers and amplifiers, always look at the RMS values, not 'peak' values. RMS is a measurement of averages and is more reliable as a measurement than peak values. A speaker can have RMS values of 200 watts and a peak value of 600 watts, an amp delivering 300 watts RMS will still do it damage.

Specifications or salesmen that insist on quoting peak values rather than RMS values are trying to sell you goods that may not necessarily be as good as those you want to buy.

A quick guide to impedance in the real world. Adding an additional pair of 8 ohm speakers to an existing pair of 8 ohm speakers in a stereo system.

A Output around 280 watts, just two speakers.

B Add another pair of speakers and output rises to 400 watts

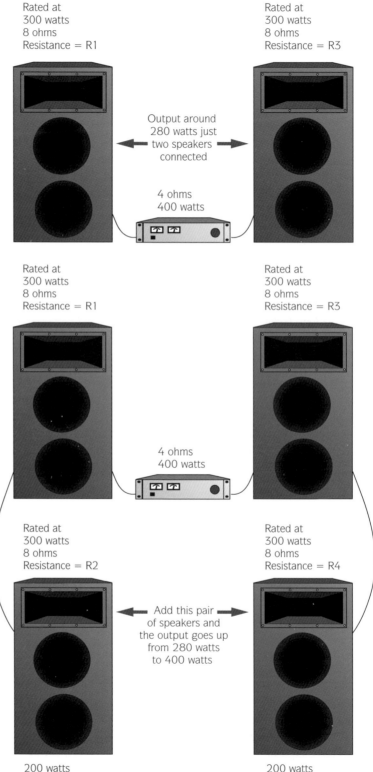

Rated at
300 watts
8 ohms
Resistance = R1

Rated at
300 watts
8 ohms
Resistance = R3

A

Output around 280 watts just two speakers connected

4 ohms
400 watts

Rated at
300 watts
8 ohms
Resistance = R1

Rated at
300 watts
8 ohms
Resistance = R3

B

4 ohms
400 watts

Rated at
300 watts
8 ohms
Resistance = R2

Rated at
300 watts
8 ohms
Resistance = R4

Add this pair of speakers and the output goes up from 280 watts to 400 watts

200 watts

200 watts

you will halve the impedance of the overall circuit so that it will now be 4 ohms. This will draw the full rated power from the amplifier, 400 watts per channel, at full tilt, 200 watts into each cabinet, within both the cabinet specification and the amplifier specification. The only trouble here may be that running the amp flat out could affect quality.

If two resistances are in line with each other, *in series*, so the output of one feeds into the input of the other, the combined resistance will be the sum total of the two resistances.

Total resistance = R1 + R2

In a parallel circuit, where the source feeds all the resistances simultaneously, the total resistance = (R1 x R2)/(R1 + R2)

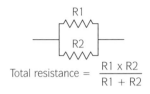

Total resistance = R1 + R2

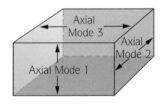

Total resistance = $\dfrac{R1 \times R2}{R1 + R2}$

Mobile — the venue

The room has not been mentioned before, yet it is as important as any other component, certainly in the mobile DJ system.

Acoustics is a deep and far ranging subject beyond the scope of this book. Suffice it to say that unless you are playing in the open air, with no reflective objects in the path of the sound, then the sound is going to be altered by the space in which it is being played. Most rooms are rectangular and, in rectangular enclosures, there are three types of acoustic resonance to be found; they are known as axial, tangential and oblique modes. The main one that concerns us is the axial mode, because this is the one that describes the behaviour of two waves going in opposite directions. As there are three axes in a rectangular room, so there will be three fundamental axial frequencies. In plain language, the sound bounces off the opposite wall back to meet itself; the size of the room and its ratio of length:width:height, will determine which frequencies and harmonics are affected. Sound travels in waves and low frequencies consist of longer waves that travel further than the shorter waves generated by high frequencies, so it is usually the bass that is affected. The results can be quite noticeable, in certain rooms there will exist a sort of underlying heavy hum, which is a particular frequency bouncing round and building up a resonance.

Here is some maths. It is for you to work out the actual wavelength of a frequency where there may be a problem in a particular room. The formula is:

C=WF
C is the speed of sound that is affected by ambient temperature
    (warmer faster, colder slower)
W is wavelength
F is frequency

Using transposition to find a wavelength, C=WF becomes W=C/F.

Let's say it's a warm room, so the speed of sound is 344 metres per second. The frequency we are interested in is 150Hz. Thus W=344/150, or a frequency of 150Hz is equivalent to a 2.29 metres wavelength. What we have is a wave like the one on the right.

This measures 2.29 metres in a complete cycle. If by chance the room you're in is 9.16m long (4 x 2.29m), have a guess which frequency will come rolling back

Axial Modes in a room.

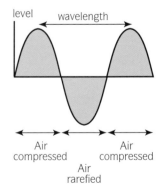

Graphical representation of a sound wave; the length is the distance from tip to tip (one complete cycle).

Tip

To understand the phenomena that these bass frequencies create in a room, nip into the kitchen, grab a roasting tray or any shallow, flat rectangular dish and fill it half full with water. Put it on a flat surface, tip it up slightly and they lay it down. The wave that comes back from the far end of the tin will usually have more power than the original one you created. You can get the same effect in a bath by getting up (from sitting/lying down) quickly. That's what happens with sound waves from your speakers in a rectangular room, but it's not just one wave going backwards and forwards, it's many.

from the far wall. It is slightly more complex than that but now you can see the idea.

In reality unless a tone generator is used, you are never going to generate a simple waveform. The 150Hz wave is going to be amongst a complex pattern of waves that make up the audio signal, but the size and shape of the room (the distance between ends) will dictate that certain frequencies will resonate in the three different axes of the rectangle. There are formulae with which you can calculate these, but as I have said, acoustics is a science that is beyond my expertise and the scope of this book. However, it *is* important that you understand that the shape and size of the room you are working in will affect the quality of your sound. You need to be aware of this, not least because it will help you to grasp the little tricks you can use to dodge potential problems.

Where I live, a popular farm restaurant was gaining so much function business that they decided to extend and build a purpose made function suite. The suite is approximately 30 metres long by 10 metres wide, and it's 3 metres high. There is a bar at one end, some plug sockets at the other, with an empty space in between. The food is lovely, the car park is great, the view over the rolling hills is fantastic, but the function room is an acoustic nightmare. The only time it gets to sound good is when everyone is up dancing, until then it is a nightmare.

The architect was so concerned about the design blending in and conforming to National Park requirements that it seems he never thought about acoustics. The building regulations department was so concerned about depth of foundations, lintel loads and fire escapes that they never thought about acoustics. The owners were so concerned about keeping the other two happy and about cost that they never thought about acoustics.

The walls are stone and plaster, there are no soft furnishings and it doesn't matter who turns up there to play and with what equipment, the sound is always terrible. Of course it isn't the music, the common denominator is the room. Ask anybody who knows anything about acoustics and they will tell you about the nightmare of sound waves bouncing around a regular sized and proportioned hard, rectangular box.

This situation is not an unusual one. I regularly work at a world famous hotel in a beautiful village – one of the best places in the UK to have a wedding reception. It is fantastic. The functions are held in a marvellous reproduction baronial hall, with rich wood panelling and a high relief plaster ceiling. It's another acoustic nightmare. This problem is very current in the mobile scene; usually anywhere a mobile DJ plays which has not been specifically designed for that usage *is* a nightmare. It doesn't matter what size the rig is or what is the quality of the components, nothing matters because the shape of the room dictates the final sound, unless you fill the room with speakers and effectively mask any reflections or reverb.

A big room with high vaulted plaster ceilings adds reverb, a long room with flat surfaces at either end creates standing waves at certain bass frequencies, like the water slopping backwards and forwards in a bath. There are endless combinations of the two. In a club, the mid and high frequency speakers are usually suspended over the dance area, with the bass speakers being fixed in a wall at floor level pointing right at the dance floor. The idea here is that the sound gets to the ears first and is soaked up against soft bodies, before it has the chance to bounce around everywhere else. This is not so in your local pub or hotel.

Here are some tips that will help you to make the best of a bad situation and get a better sound from these nightmare rooms. These tips are based on the principles that hard surfaces reflect sounds, soft surfaces absorb sound and when sound waves bounce off a hard flat surface, the angle of reflection will be the same as the angle of incidence. For the purposes of these tips, it will be assumed that we are not dealing with exceptionally large venues where phasing, or diffraction, are issues.

In a long rectangular or square room with a fairly low ceiling:

• Don't put the speakers on stands.
• Don't point the speakers straight ahead, turn them slightly so the sound is not bouncing straight off the opposite wall.
• Set up in a corner, or slightly off centre, so you are playing across the room diagonally.
• Turn the bass down.
• Close the curtains.
• Keep the volume down until the room gets busy.
• Buy a Behringer Ultracurve or a DBX DriveRack PA™.

In a big high room with vaulted plaster ceilings:

• Don't put the speakers on stands.
• Don't point the speakers straight ahead, turn them slightly so the sound is not bouncing straight off the opposite wall.
• Set up in a corner, or slightly off centre, so you are playing across the room diagonally.

Side view

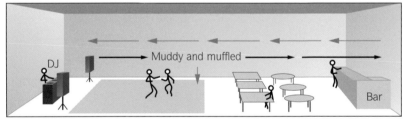

Speakers on stands pointing directly down the room are a recipe for disaster.

Top view

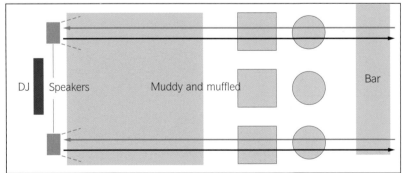

- Turn the bass down.
- Turn the treble down.
- Close the curtains.
- Keep the volume down until the room gets busy.
- Buy a Behringer Ultracurve or a DBX DriveRack PA.

Now I know that an acoustics expert would probably baulk at the suggestions I have made. These are not ideal solutions by any means but in the real world, with limited resources they are a partial fix to an everyday problem. By their nature, these rooms aren't going to be full of soft furnishings or irregular shapes to absorb the sound and no matter how good a room is, it is always going to alter the sound in some way. A professional DJ should know what to do to compensate.

The only way to hear what your system *really* sounds like is to get out in a field somewhere, with nothing in the way, or in a tent, in a field. The rest of the time will be a compromise. I have seen DJs with the best equipment that money can buy, running round oblong boxes in a sweat, scratching their heads and wondering why their JBLs, up on stands, sound like JCBs. It's the room, you learn how to deal with it.

This is all proved when you see how an active system like the HK is set up, the bass bins sit on the floor the tops sit on poles inserted into the bins, usually angled downwards so the sound doesn't fly straight across the room and bounce back off the opposing wall. Even so, do set them up off centre.

Side view

For optimum sound, set up in a corner and keep the speakers at a low level.

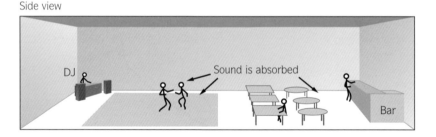

Top view

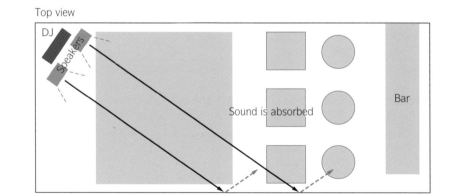

Equipment profile

While we are not here to plug equipment, if I feel that a piece of kit is worth sin-gling out for special mention, I shall do it. Frequently, peripheral equipment that is not a major item in the signal chain is overlooked, but the ability some of this equipment has to enhance the quality of the sound output should not be underes-timated.

Behringer Ultracurve Pro DEQ2496, Behringer Ultracurve Pro DSP8024 or DSP8000

The Behringer Ultracurve is such a piece of kit. It is a 'digital' graphic equalizer and a lot more besides. Amongst other things, it can identify the acoustic anomalies occurring in a room and EQ them out, in effect 'flattening' the room. The unit gen-erates and plays out pink noise which it then 'listens to' via its companion micro-phone, the ECM 8000, to see how the room has affected the sound output (it acts as a spectrum analyzer). The EQ curve is then adjusted, to alter the sound output to give the reflected sound a flat response, all based on the room's dynamics. The result is stored in a scene memory. The preferred EQ settings can then be super-imposed on the flattened response and stored. Every time you play in that room you can call it up.

The Ultracurve is neither cheap nor expensive, when compared with normal good quality graphic equalizers, but it is a mobile piece of kit specifically designed for the job. When installation companies fit out a club with sound equipment they will, as part of the commissioning process, follow this exact procedure. They play pink noise out through the sound system and then, using a spectrum analyzer, they will analyze the frequency response of the room and see how it alters the sound. Manual alterations will be made to the graphic equalizer, until there is either a flat response, or the response curve is as desired. Then they will put a locking cover over the graphic so that DJs don't mess it up.

A mobile DJ with an Ultracurve can do that every night and can even have dif-ferent settings for when the room is empty or full. There is no point installing an Ultracurve in clubs, because there should be no need to reset the EQ, unless an alteration is made to the room or new equipment brought in. This is only one of the Ultracurve's many functions, it can be used to eliminate feedback and it is also a creative tool which can be software updated and MIDI controllable. Read all about it on the Behringer website, detailed in the Resources section. If you can't stretch to a new one, check out eBay and *Sound on Sound* magazine.

Aphex Aural Exciter® Type C2 with Big Bottom™ or Aphex Aural Exciter® 204 with Optical Big Bottom™

Another piece of kit worthy of special mention is the Aphex. I have tried not to let personal feelings about inanimate objects colour my objective view of how a DJ should operate, but in the case of the above I have to become emotional. I've also said that DJing, in whichever sphere of the discipline you are involved, has got to be about the music. The dynamics of playing back recorded music are totally dif-ferent from those of live music, so ideally, the use of EQ should be minimal wher-ever possible.

Many years ago, I was at a friend's house where he had an excellent hi fi sys-tem. We were listening to a new Nina Simone album (on vinyl). Well, the hairs on

The latest version of the Aphex Aural Exciter – the model 204.

the back of my neck weren't just tingling, they were running up and down jabbing me with hot needles. I'm not a zealous Nina Simone fan, but the sound of this lady's voice on this album was amazing. I read the album sleeve and saw a little note saying that the vocals have been recorded using an Aphex Aural Exciter®. Further investigation revealed that an Aural Exciter® was a physcoacoustic something or other, you couldn't buy them, you could only hire them and they were expensive.

Fast-forward 20 years. I have been dragged out of retirement. The sound system I use is OK, the rooms I get to play in are horrible, the money isn't bad but what I am looking for all the time is a way to improve my sound, to improve my quality of delivery. The crowd probably won't notice and probably don't care, but I do – after all it's got to be about the music.

CDs, for all their other qualities of sonic purity, lightweight, capacity and ease of use, seem to somehow lack the warmth (noise) of vinyl. The amplifier I use is very good, very clinical, as are my speakers. But the sound is not warm. If I add any bass, it becomes thumpy, heavy and oppressive – still not warm. By chance, I was surfing through eBay and came across an auction for a second hand Aphex Aural Exciter® Type C2 with Big Bottom™. Now there are quite a few types available second hand, but this is the one with 'Big Bottom' that, according to the blurb is best for general PA and disco work. They are normally quite expensive but this one wasn't, I bid for it and won the auction. A week later it arrived from Germany and went straight into my rack, after the mixer in front of the graphic and amps.

It arrived with the best handbook I have ever seen, not only for its own operation, but also for some general principles of audio connecting and performance. I followed the instructions and the first time I used it, it blew me away. I was in, possibly, the worst room in the world, but my volume was down, the EQ on my mixer was flat, my graphic equalizer no longer resembled a Big Dipper. I didn't have to turn the bass up to add warmth and my rig has stayed like that ever since. It is the strangest thing, the rig sounds loud when it isn't particularly, there's plenty of body in the bass without it being thumpy and oppressive and there is sweetness to the highs where there was rasping before.

The manual describes the functioning very well. The superior sound quality, particularly the bass that now emanates from my little rig, is well worth those few pounds I paid for the unit. The difference is most noticeable when I use my little Cerwin Vegas in a small room, but it should be said that the superior quality, whichever combination of rig I use, is more than evident.

The Type C2s are available, second hand, from the *Sound On Sound* website or eBay, especially in Germany, because Aphex have brought out a new model. If you are lucky enough to track one down, make sure it has a manual, because although it's simple to operate you need to know where to start. I guarantee you too will notice a great difference in your sound immediately, it is like having a sub woofer on your system. Anywhere that plays recorded music in any format would benefit from having one of these units in the signal chain. A downside? Well, it can require fine adjustment between tracks, as each track is slightly different, to maintain its equilibrium; but if anything improves my sound, it is more than welcome.

DBX DriveRack™ PA

Added to our list of gear to get excited about is the DBX DriveRack™ PA. Why? Because it does what the Ultracurve does, as well as provide a variety of crossover output options, stereo compression, so you don't overload the signal chain, and, if you don't have an Aphex, a sub harmonic thingy which enhances the bass sound. At around £400 it is not cheap but then if you add together the cost of an Aphex, an Ultracurve, a good stereo compressor, and a two or three way crossover, and the leads required to connect them all together, suddenly it doesn't seem so expen-

sive. The only misgiving is that if one thing goes wrong, you have lost them all, but modern electronics is so reliable, and with all due respects to other manufacturers of speaker control systems, this is a DBX unit, and DBX are one of the top echelon of manufacturers.

DBX DriveRack™ PA

As with the Ultracurve you can use the unit to generate pink noise and then listen to the speaker output through it's companion microphone and feed the result through a real time analyser. So in essence it does what the other two items in our list do, with exactly the same outcome. The added bonus, and really good thing about the DriveRack PA™, are the crossover options, you can go stereo, bi amp, tri amp and on. It adds in versatility and means, you can upgrade your rig as far as amplification and speakers go, even temporarily, while still using the DriveRack PA™ to control everything. Oh, and of course only one rack space used up, and a lot fewer connecting wires.

Lighting

Most club DJ booths will have some lighting to enable you to see your 12 inch singles (you can't work if it's pitch black). On the road, however, always carry a small lamp for use behind the turntables, especially if you are using CDs on which the written details can be very tiny. There is not much to say about sound to light. If you are a club DJ, someone else will look after the light system.

If you are a mobile DJ, the rules are: don't use anything which switches itself on/off automatically, stay away from dimmer packs or inductive loads (which can pull current through your mains system) and unless your job is doing really big gigs, in which case you will have a lighting crew anyway, don't get over involved with lights. Buy self contained units, which dance about on their own to the music, two maybe three units will be enough.

Big lighting rigs for mobile DJs are ego trips, no one ever says, after a mobile DJ show, 'wasn't the lighting great?' If they are going to offer praise, they will say 'great music, great sound'. You can't dance to lights.

The best lighting rig I have ever seen, in a small venue, belonged to a North Wales husband and wife singing duo called Penny Black. It was absolutely breathtaking, but then so was their act. Their sound was incredible but, more importantly, they had an audience who watched them and were able to appreciate the complete show. Had the same light show accompanied a DJ, it would have been unnoticed; the sound system they used was the real star. In speaking to them, it was obvious that, despite the fabulous lighting set up, their concern was getting the sound right. Which tells you all you need to know really.

Connections

There are a variety of connections used in the audio/video industry, a variety of standards and specifications that are used to ensure compatibility between devices. These are scattered throughout the book but some of the most common ones are condensed in this little section for you, with brief explanations of where they are found.

The RCA/phono plug. Usually found in domestic equipment, to interconnect composite video (yellow) and left and right stereo sound signals (red and black/white). They are also found on professional equipment, where stereo 'line' inputs and outputs are required and on turntables to connect to an RIAA/phono input on a mixer. The recent trend on analogue connections is for OFC (oxygen free copper) cable to be used, this is usually directional, so the signal should 'flow' in the direction indicated by the arrows on the wire casing. The RCA/phono lead represents an unbalanced connection in the unity gain chart (see pic overleaf).

The mono 6.35mm jack plug (phone jack) is a standard and long-lived connection between devices and instruments. It is an unbalanced connection in the unity gain chart. It will be found connecting guitars to amplifiers, amplifiers to speakers, all over the place.

The stereo 6.35mm jack plug (phone jack) is also a standard and long-lived connection. If it is used as a stereo connection, then it is unbalanced in the unity gain chart. It can however also be used as a balanced connection in a mono balanced environment.

The XLR (Cannon) plug/socket. This is another established connection, it can be used as a stereo connection (unbalanced), a mono connection (unbalanced) and as a balanced mono connection. In some cases it can also be used for power. It is most commonly found as a socket on mixers where a microphone input is required, so it will also be found as a plug socket combination at the base of the microphone and as a plug on the end of the microphone cable. In these cases, it is usually wired as a balanced line to minimize interference. It will also be found as a socket, as a balanced master output, from most professional equipment. It can also be wired to a stereo jack plug/socket and still be a balanced line.

Standard RCA/phono/cinch plug.

Mono 6.35mm standard jack plug.

Stereo or mono balanced 6.35mm standard jack plug.

XLR plug (also available as a chassis mount version).

XLR socket (also available as a chassis mount version).

The SPDIF plug (75 ohm coax) digital interface is an RCA/phono lead, it can be yellow or black. The only difference between these and normal phono leads is that they are sold singly, rather than in a left or right pair and the line impedance is stated to be 75 ohm. There are no bandwidth concerns, because the lead is transmitting digital data, not audio, so enhanced cable quality is not an issue; so no OFC cable here, just normal cable that complies with the 75 ohm standard. Another 75 ohm digital interface exists as a BNC connector, it is basically the same connection just using different termination.

The AES/EBU digital interface (110 ohm) looks suspiciously like an XLR/Cannon lead. That's because it is, as with the SPDIF the main issue is one of line impedance, in this case 110 ohm is the standard. It carries no audio signals, just data.

The TOS Link/optical digital interface. This is found connecting digital devices, along with, or as an alternative to, the SPDIF and AES/EBU interface. Since there are no impedance issues as the cable is fibre optic, this connection will be found on domestic equipment such as CDRs, MiniDiscs™ and in a mini form on portable MiniDiscs™. It carries no audio signals, just data at the speed of light.

The 5 pin DIN MIDI Interface. This is used to connect MIDI devices together; it actually started life as a catch-all audio connection many years ago, but its fragility and awkwardness made it difficult to use and easy to break. So it became the standard MIDI connection; it carries no audio signals, just data.

There are actually two miniature sizes of stereo jack plug, the 3.5mm and 2.5mm, as well as the 4.5mm bantam jack plug. The 3.5mm stereo jack plug is found on computer sound cards and Walkman type devices, where space is an issue. There are leads and numerous converters available to take the 3.5mm jack plug to a full sized stereo jack plug, or two phonos or two 6.35mm mono jack plugs. It is an unbalanced connector on the unity gain chart and unlike its full sized cousin, it cannot be adapted to do a balanced line job.

The Speakon™ plug is the standard for speaker connection and is commonly found as a socket on all new speakers. It is expensive, so care must be taken; you don't want to tread on this too much.

Binding posts are found on the backs of certain amplifiers, certainly the American made ones, like Peaveys and Crowns. These will take either bare wire to whatever the speaker connection is, jack, XLR, or Speakon™ or banana plugs, which are essentially binding posts that plug into binding posts, to whatever is at the other end. Banana plugs are very popular stateside they offer a convenient and easy fix, are cheap, easy to fit up and they plug into each other, piggyback style. A word of warning if you use banana plugs or indeed any bare wire fixing ensure that the wire does not go across to the other terminal, that is a short circuit, and respect the wiring convention i.e. red to red and black to black or brown wire to red post and blue wire to black post. Also if you piggyback banana plugs remember not to exceed the impedance rating of the amp (see section on impedance).

There are converters and connectors available for all the analogue connections as well as for some digital ones. Care has to be taken when using a converter on a balanced line circuit for obvious reasons. If the line is balanced, it is to minimize possible interference, when the line is converted from balanced to unbalanced that precaution is overridden. Worse than that, if the balanced line is terminated wrongly, 6dB of the signal can be lost and phase problems can arise.

5 pin DIN plug, there are other configurations and sizes, this being the most common.

Two pole Speakon™ plug.

Two pole Speakon™ socket.

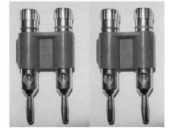

Banana plugs are cheap, easy to fit up and they plug into each other, piggyback style.

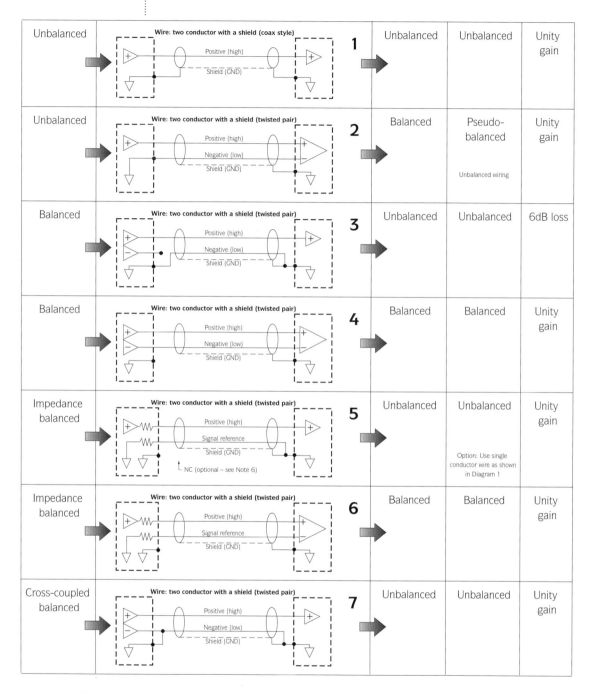

Unbalanced	Wire: two conductor with a shield (coax style) Positive (high) Shield (GND)	**1**	Unbalanced	Unbalanced	Unity gain
Unbalanced	Wire: two conductor with a shield (twisted pair) Positive (high) Negative (low) Shield (GND)	**2**	Balanced	Pseudo-balanced Unbalanced wiring	Unity gain
Balanced	Wire: two conductor with a shield (twisted pair) Positive (high) Negative (low) Shield (GND)	**3**	Unbalanced	Unbalanced	6dB loss
Balanced	Wire: two conductor with a shield (twisted pair) Positive (high) Negative (low) Shield (GND)	**4**	Balanced	Balanced	Unity gain
Impedance balanced	Wire: two conductor with a shield (twisted pair) Positive (high) Signal reference Shield (GND) NC (optional – see Note 6)	**5**	Unbalanced	Unbalanced Option: Use single conductor wire as shown in Diagram 1	Unity gain
Impedance balanced	Wire: two conductor with a shield (twisted pair) Positive (high) Signal reference Shield (GND)	**6**	Balanced	Balanced	Unity gain
Cross-coupled balanced	Wire: two conductor with a shield (twisted pair) Positive (high) Negative (low) Shield (GND)	**7**	Unbalanced	Unbalanced	Unity gain

Unity gain chart showing how connections
affect gain structure.

Balanced and unbalanced connector wiring standards

3 pin XLR	6.35 mm TRS Phono	Standard wiring convention (balanced)
Pin 1	Sleeve	ground/shield (earth, screen)
Pin 2	Tip	positive (signal, high, hot)
Pin 3	Ring	negative (signal reference, return, low, common)

6.35 mm TRS Phono	Phono (RCA)	Standard wiring convention (unbalanced)
Tip	Centre pin	positive (signal)
Sleeve	Outer	ground/shield (and signal reference/return)

Wiring a balanced and an unbalanced jack plug.

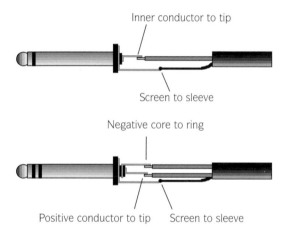

Inner conductor to tip

Screen to sleeve

Negative core to ring

Positive conductor to tip   Screen to sleeve

**Wiring an unbalanced
6.35 mm jack**
Using a single conductor shielded cable, terminate the positive (signal) conductor to tip, and the screen (ground/signal reference) to sleeve.

If you want to use two-conductor shielded cable, terminate the positive conductor to tip, tie the negative conductor and the shield together and terminate to the sleeve.

**Wiring a balanced
6.35 mm jack**
Using a two-conductor screened cable, terminate the positive (signal) conductor to tip, the negative (signal reference) conductor to ring, and the screen (ground) to sleeve.

Other equipment

There is so much equipment available of such high quality, that it is difficult to do anything other than generalize. The tip has got to be, see what other people are using and ask them what they think, they will soon tell you what is up to the job or otherwise. No piece of equipment is perfect, personal preference and experience play a big part in people's decisions. You can learn to use anything proficiently, given time. Visit shows and showrooms, have a go on things. If you are buying, bring the choice down to three or four items on paper and then go and try them out.

As more and more DJs become 'producers', the variety and complexity of the equipment they experience increase significantly. It is not uncommon now for DJs to use samplers, sound modules/keyboards or sequencers and effects as part of a live set. More and more DJs are becoming the musical artists. Certainly the career path for DJs has altered radically over the last 10–15 years. An increasing number of re mix engineers and producers were previously DJs, rather than musicians, so the knowledge of equipment amongst DJs has risen accordingly. I hope that the basics are covered adequately in here and that some of the mystique surrounding that oh-so complicated control panel has been removed.

Sound basics 5

OK. This is the boring bit – or maybe not. One thing is for sure, acting on this information will make you stand out from the crowd. You will sound better and be more confident in your ability, having read and understood this section. This is also the area where you guys have got it so good, because the sound quality now is so much better than it was, even just ten years ago. There is a lot of stuff to know. What we have tried to do here is draw the line between being informative and useful for you and being scientific. Unfortunately, there are some physics that you need to know, to keep you and your equipment safe and in good working order, but we will try to keep that to a minimum.

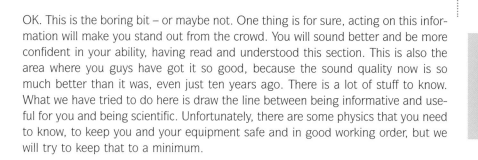

Info

Dynamic range is the difference between the quietest sound that a piece of equipment can reproduce (noise floor) and the loudest signal a piece of equipment can reproduce without distorting.

Dynamic range, noise, rumble and crosstalk

When an audio signal is amplified it is made louder. If there is extraneous noise in that audio signal that is made louder too. In the days of turntables that had a rumble figure of say –30dB, when the signal they produced was amplified, turntable noise, which consists of hums and rumbles, started coming from the speakers. Those of you old enough to remember cassette decks, will also remember Dolby and dbx patented noise reduction systems, designed to stop cassettes hissing. In the old analogue world, everything made a noise, and noise and hum were a fact of life and a sound system's worst enemies. In the digital world, it's a completely different story. Dynamic range is directly related to the range of binary digits, or bit rate employed, of the digital system. In fact 6dB of dynamic range equates to 1 bit, so a 16 bit digital system, like CDs, has a theoretical dynamic range of 96dB. So what exactly is dynamic range? Well in it's simplest form, dynamic range is the difference between the quietest sound that a piece of equipment can reproduce (noise floor) and the loudest signal a piece of equipment can reproduce without distorting. When we refer to headroom, we are referring to the difference between the level we are operating at and the equipment's limit, simply how much room is left. Every piece of equipment will quote a signal to noise ratio, which is its effective dynamic range and headroom when nothing is happening. In a digital world quiet is the norm.

If you look at any audio equipment specification, you will always see figures like hum, crosstalk, signal to noise ratio. These figures tell you how much noise, or the level of interference, the item they refer to contributes to the signal it is trying to process or deliver. When compared with the spec of a Garrard SP25 turntable, a CD player, any CD player, is not even on the same planet. The signal to noise ratio of an ordinary CD player is around –96dB (16bit system). Compare that with the

Figure 5.01
A graphical representation of dynamic range, noise floor and headroom.

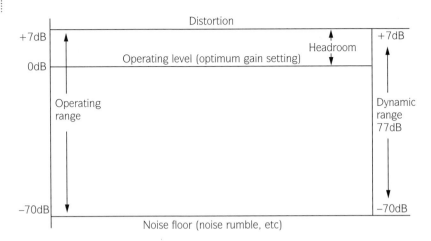

Channel A   Channel B

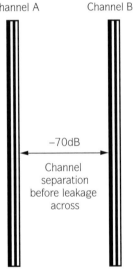

−70dB

Channel
separation
before leakage
across

Figure 5.02
Crosstalk. Interference between or across channels.

rumble figure, of say −30dB on old turntables, or −56dB (IEC 98A Unweighted) −78dB (IEC 98A Weighted) on a good quality professional turntable, like a Technics SL1200 Mk II, before it makes noise and the difference is more appreciable.

At first glance, that's nearly half as good again as the best turntable, but that's not the way decibels (dBs) are measured. They are not measured in increments of one, but on a logarithmic scale. An increase of 6dB is not six units but a doubling, so to reduce the signal to noise ratio threshold from −96dB to, at best, −78dB, which is a reduction of 18 dB, is effectively making the −78dB turntable three times as noisy as the CD player. In other words, CD players are three times quieter than the best turntables, eleven times quieter than the old Garrards; at 2000 watts RMS that's a lot of quiet. You'll now understand in advance why you will get such a hard time over setting the gain structure later on.

Just as an aside, to make things complicated, there are two dB scales that we are interested in. One relates to voltage and one relates to power. An increase of 6dB is a doubling of voltage, whereas an increase of 3dB is a doubling of power. Is this confusing? Well, it's down to mathematical formulae, which you don't really need to know. But, to give you a practical example: if the VU meter shows −6dB and you push the volume control up until it shows 0dB (an increase of 6dB), you will have doubled the voltage at the output. If you stood in front of the speakers with a measuring device giving a reading of 96dBA when the VU meter was show-ing −6dB when the level was pushed up by 6dB to 0dB you would, in our perfectly performing system, now be measuring 99dBA in front of the speakers, but the sound would be twice as loud.

We are not going to go into decibels any further, but to give you an idea of a decibel in the normal world, we have put together a list of everyday sounds and where they figure on the scale of measurement by decibel (dBA), together with some idea of the recommended levels/times of exposure to loud noise that are gen-erally regarded as harmful.

Now this improved quality is taken for granted, it makes setting up a lot easier, the absence of any significant noise from the CD players and mixer reaching the amp is virtually guaranteed, unless the gain structure is wrongly set up. If the gain struc-ture is correctly set everything will sound clean and great and with the volume up the output sounds good. So let's take more than a quick look at setting gain structure.

Average pressure levels of common sounds

130	
	Jet aircraft taking off
120	
110	Pneumatic drill at 1 m
	Wood-working machinery
100	Discos
90	Symphony orchestra playing *fff*
80	Outdoor p.a. system (peaks)
	Vacuum cleaner at 1 m
70	Inside cruising motor coach
	Speaking voice at 1 m
60	General office
	Orchestral woodwind solos
50	Whisper at 1 m
	Orchestra (strings) playing *ppp*
40	
	Quiet living room
30	
20	
	Quiet countryside
10	
0	Threshold of hearing

Figure 5.03 (left)
The decibel in the real world

Figure 5.04
Sound level exposure times before hearing damage starts.

dBA	Time
90	8 hours
93	4 hours
96	2 hours
99	1 hour
102	30 minutes
105	15 minutes
108	7.5 minutes
111	3.75 minutes

Gain structure

Gain structure is the name given to the relative settings of the levels on outputs from, and inputs to, various channels and devices in the signal/sound chain. Matched outputs and inputs between device stages give better, quieter, more efficient circuits, as will properly configured connections (also called unity gain) between physical components. This is what we want. Electrical circuits carrying electrical signals that will be converted into sound need to be free from interference. Interfere with the electrical signal and that also interferes with the sound. When outputs/inputs are matched and the gain structure is correctly set, everything is running at its optimum level.

The gain structure diagram is exactly the same as the dynamic range illustration (Figure 5.01), except the ideal operating level becomes, surprisingly, the optimum setting for the gain.

Below is an extract from the Output terminal table from an early Pioneer DJM500 mixer manual.

Output terminal (Output level/impedance
MASTER OUT 1 (RCA).....................0dBV (1V)/1k◘

Roughly translated, this means that the mixer's optimum delivery, through this output, will be at the 0dB setting on the master VU meter, equal to 1 volt into an input, across which it will meet 1k◘ (1000 ohms) of impedance. It has other outputs in addition to this one, which are optimally suited to other inputs. Master out 2 for example reads as follows:

MASTER OUT 2 (XLR).....................4dBm (1.23V)/600ᴑ

This is what master out 2 delivers into its ideal input, when the VU meter is showing 0dB. These can be physically measured using a test CD and a multimeter. The Pioneer, in common with other mixers has a master level adjustment control so the levels can be set exactly.

So the input specification of the next device in the signal chain determines which output on the mixer is used for optimum delivery of the signal to that device.

In the real world gain structure is everything. On the front of the mixer we use in our examples, there is, beside each channel's tone controls (or EQ section), a little strip of LEDs, this is the channel VU meter. Now you may think the level signal coming in here is controlled by the fader; it is not. The level of the signal going *out* of the channel to the master section is determined by the position of the fader. The trim control situated at the top of the channel strip controls the input signal to the channel, and what is seen in the VU meter is independent of the fader setting. The fader controls the percentage of that input signal which is allowed through the mixer channel to the output or master section.

All this is common to most mixers, the one main difference being when there are a limited number of VU meters on the mixer and the channel being measured has to be assigned to them. In our example, there is also a separate pair of LED VU meters marked master level, which measure the level of the signal leaving the mixer; this level is controlled by the master fader. When the input signal is set by the trim control so that the VU is rising to the 0 mark, the input to the channel is at its optimum, where sound quality is at its best, noise at its least and everything in the garden is rosy.

When the channel fader is at the top, pushing its 0dB input signal to the master section and when the master fader is set so that the signal going out of the mixer is measured on the VU at 0dB, the master output section is functioning at its optimum level. In the same way, so is the channel and additionally this tells us that the output of the mixer at master out 1 should be as shown in the box; so should the output at master out 2 be as shown in the box.

I can't stress the importance of gain structure enough, it is so vital yet simple. If you aspire to be a club DJ, seamlessly segueing the top dance tunes to a 5000 strong crowd in a hangar somewhere, the only way to make your mixes invisible is by the correct implementation of gain structure – even, if until now, you didn't know what it was called. Similarly, if you are a mobile DJ and want to get a reputation for good quality delivery and you want your equipment to live long and function normally, gain structure will become your creed. It's a good habit to get into and one that will serve you well. Resist the temptation to get more volume by sacrificing gain structure. Once the gain structure is set, through the system, the amp is the only place to go for more volume.

Info

If you aspire to be a club DJ, seamlessly segueing the top dance tunes to a 5000 strong crowd in a hangar somewhere, the only way to make your mixes invisible is by the correct implementation of gain structure.

LED VU meters measure the level of input into the channel after EQ.

Channel Trim controls. Control the amount of signal coming into the mixer.

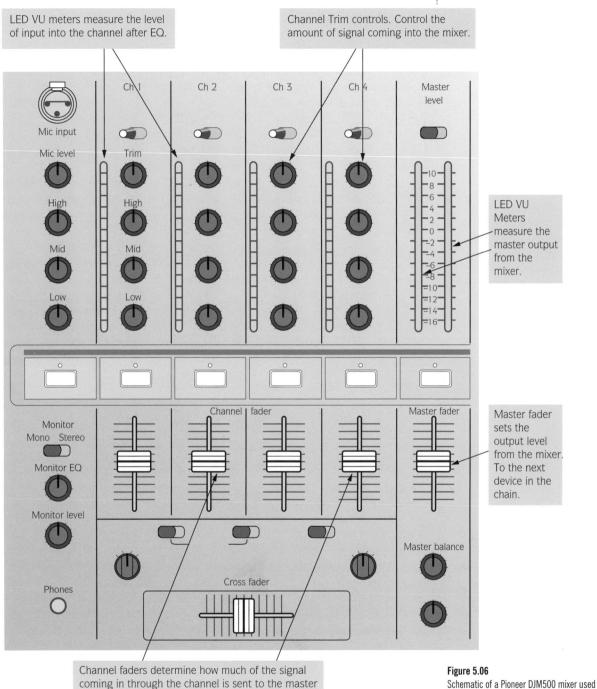

LED VU Meters measure the master output from the mixer.

Master fader sets the output level from the mixer. To the next device in the chain.

Channel faders determine how much of the signal coming in through the channel is sent to the master section for output.

Figure 5.06
Schematic of a Pioneer DJM500 mixer used to illustrate gain settings.

Figure 5.07
Master fader too high, pushing distortion out (gain structure compromised) see Figure 5.08.

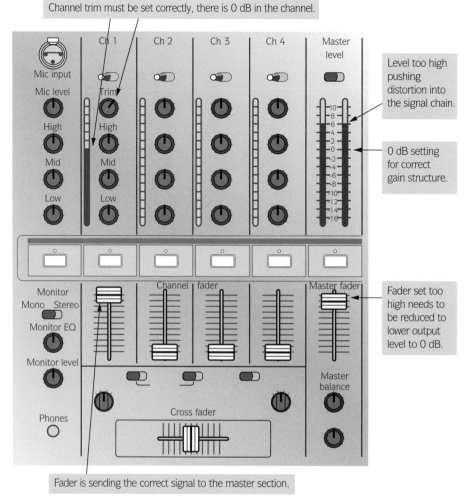

Channel trim must be set correctly, there is 0 dB in the channel.

Level too high pushing distortion into the signal chain.

0 dB setting for correct gain structure.

Fader set too high needs to be reduced to lower output level to 0 dB.

Fader is sending the correct signal to the master section.

Figure 5.08
Graphical representation of Figure 5.07 (based on master output from mixer). Mixer output too high – into distortion, which is being sent to the next device in the signal chain.

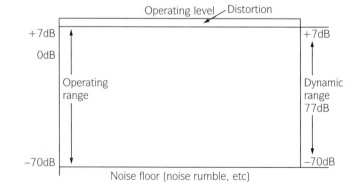

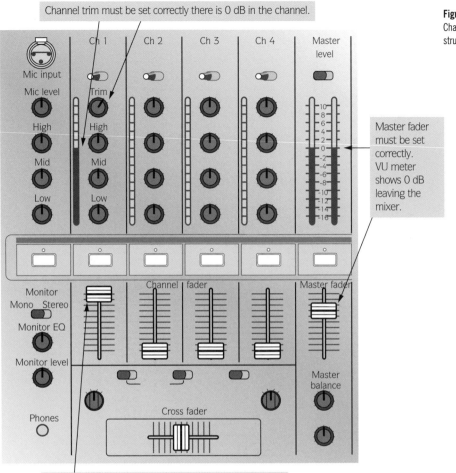

Channel trim must be set correctly there is 0 dB in the channel.

Fader is sending the correct signal to the master section.

Figure 5.09
Channel is at 0dB, master is at 0dB (gain structure OK) see Figure 5.10.

Master fader must be set correctly. VU meter shows 0 dB leaving the mixer.

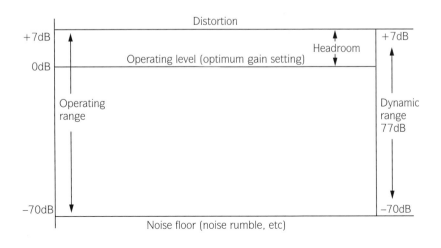

Figure 5.10
Graphical representation of gain structure when the component is set at its optimum operating level.

Figure 5.11
Channel trim set too low, master pushed up to compensate (gain structure compromised) see Figure 5.12.

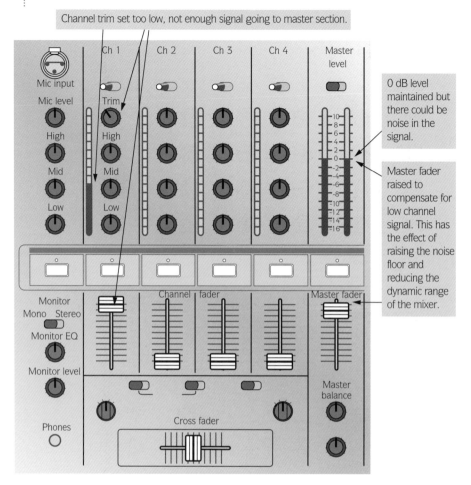

Channel trim set too low, not enough signal going to master section.

0 dB level maintained but there could be noise in the signal.

Master fader raised to compensate for low channel signal. This has the effect of raising the noise floor and reducing the dynamic range of the mixer.

Figure 5.12
Graphical representation of Figure 5.11 (based on master output from mixer). With the trim level set too low the master level is increased to compensate, this amplifies the noise as well and has the effect of raising the noise floor therefore reducing the overall dynamic range.

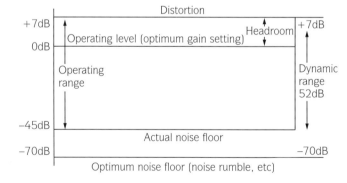

Info

It doesn't matter what the salesman says, don't even get tempted to buy a mixer that doesn't have channel trim controls

Channel trim set too high possibility of distortion being sent to the master section.

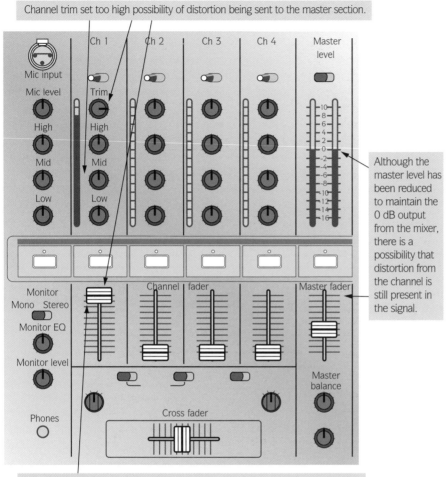

Figure 5.13
Channel trim set too high, master pulled down to compensate (gain structure compromised) see Figure 5.14.

Although the master level has been reduced to maintain the 0 dB output from the mixer, there is a possibility that distortion from the channel is still present in the signal.

Even if this fader is pulled down there may still be input distortion in the channel.

Info

It doesn't matter what the salesman says, don't even get tempted to buy a mixer that doesn't have channel trim controls.

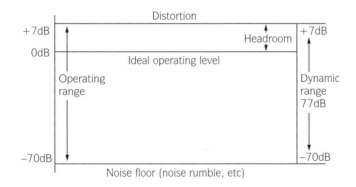

Figure 5.14
Graphical representation of Figure 5.13 (based on master output from mixer). On the surface everything looks OK but, if there is distortion present in the overloaded channel signal, it will be passed through the master section into the next device in signal chain.

One last time

If you were to undertake any course in professional sound engineering, one of the main topics that would be covered would be gain structure and unity gain. The premise is very simple, it is the duty of a professional to get the best signal possible from the equipment being used, without any additional noise or distortion being added.

It doesn't matter which type of mixer you use, how big, or how expensive it is, all that matters is that the gain structure is set properly. Which means no EQ, no effects, channel trim set to allow maximum signal through fader, 0dB, output set to maximum, 0dB and whatever comes later has got to be right because it started right. If the later addition of EQ, especially bass, in the channel boosts the signal, turn the trim control down to maintain 0dB and the gain structure. It's very simple and very reassuring and works irrespective of make or model of equipment, or fashion or style.

Once you have this very basic idea mastered, everything else becomes easier. If the VU meters are slapping up into the red area on a constant basis, that will be delivering distortion to the next section in the sound chain. Whatever happens from then on will sound bad because of that distortion. The red flashing VU lights jumping up and down may look spectacular in the dark but they say that the operator is a prat. There is a little headroom in the system, so there is no need to be paranoid about going above 0dB, but keep an eye on it. With every track you cue, set the gain to 0dB in the channel and it will be hard to go wrong.

The other important factor to mention here is line and impedance matching. I'm going to resist the urge to reproduce schematics and specs and go through phase cancellation; all I'm going to state is the obvious, which is:

If you are a club DJ, you have to assume that the system will have been installed and is maintained by a competent team of professionals, which means you don't have to worry about these matters, apart from the gain structure of the mixer, which is under your direct control.

If you are a mobile DJ, you will know what sort of leads you are using, i.e. balanced or unbalanced and whether they are high or low impedance. You will have fitted the appropriate leads, wired in the correct configuration, as specified in the manuals, between the components of the system. The appropriate rated outputs will be connected to the appropriate rated inputs and the system components will be compatible with each other and 'fit' together. If you are not sure just check, the manuals will tell you everything you need to know.

Equalization

What is equalization? Well, irrespective of various theories, it's a bit like the advert which says 'It does what is says on the tin'. Equalization is using electrical devices to modify the amplitude/frequency response in a reproducing system to give flat overall characteristics. In other words, to make the sound heard equal to that recorded and intended to be reproduced. Usually, owing to the properties of the space in which it is being played, the sound is not as it should be.

Most DJs' reaction to this situation is to turn up the treble and bass, irrespective of room size and shape – that is not equalization. The first thing to remember

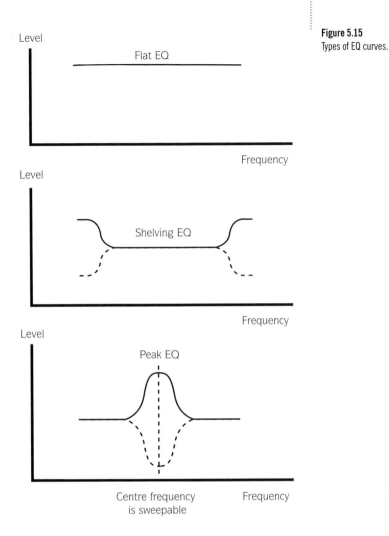

Figure 5.15
Types of EQ curves.

is to use as little EQ as possible, ideally the settings should all be flat (no gain or cut), but a little gain or cut may be applied to compensate for the room or, increasingly, for creative reasons. A good way to check on the room characteristics without fancy measuring equipment, is to pick up a mic, flatten the EQ on the mic channel, then talk down it and see how you sound. If you sound like Barry White with a cold, you've got a bass-y room, (assuming of course you don't usually sound like Barry White with a cold), if you sound like Leapy Lee with a high pitched stutter then the opposite is true.

The EQ controls on most DJ mixers are usually 'shelving type controls'. These typically affect a band of frequencies within a particular spectrum of the sound signal and are used for applying boost and cut across a band of frequencies, up to a point where the boost or cut levels out (shelves). For example, the low shelving EQ control may start around 100 Hz, the mid around 1 kHz, the high around 10 kHz. When the controls are used they affect all the frequencies between a range starting at that frequency. It is common nowadays for all EQ to be at least three band – low, mid and high. Professional sound mixers will commonly have four or five

Figure 5.16
Response curves and frequency overlaps of a graphic equalizer.

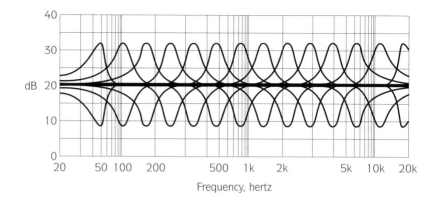

band parametric EQ controls, with a thing called variable Q and sweep type controls with adjustable frequency centres.

Most DJ systems, nowadays, both mobile and fixed, will have a graphic equalizer installed. This is a finer and more accurate type of frequency manipulation than the shelving EQ's fitted to the mixer. It uses the principle of a swept EQ based on a centre frequency; the sweep around the frequency centre is tightly controlled and so only a very limited range of frequencies is affected. Sometimes if you are doing a sound check in an empty room which has been pre EQ'd, set and locked and it sounds strange, the room has been EQ'd when full of people and the engineers have set the graphic accordingly. If the graphic has been preset, you can bet it has been done to compensate for room anomalies and get the flattest sound in spite of them.

The chances are, if the graphic has been preset, it will be locked away so you can't interfere with it. If it's open and you are expected to set it by ear, then here are some easy instructions to follow. Setting up a graphic for a disco or club is based on top and bottom, the room will accentuate the final sound but the general rule of thumb is:

- always start with the EQ flat
- roll off at the bottom end of the frequency spectrum to eliminate rumble and mic handling noise,
- then boost the bass slightly and
- reduce up to the 1kHz mark, cutting 1kHz and then gently applying boost to the higher frequencies, rolling off the very high ones that only children and dogs can hear. The ideal graphic EQ curve is said to look like Figure 5.17.

Figure 5.17
The alleged perfect EQ curve for a 'disco'.

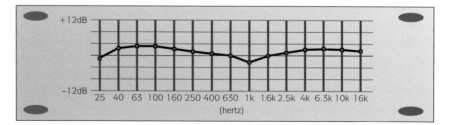

In reality, it can look like anything, but since we are not all in a financial position to own the equipment (Behringer Ultracurve or or DBX DriveRack™) which allows us to analyze every room we play in, we have to guess it. In clubs, the room will have been measured, in fact it will probably have been designed with acoustics in mind. Not so the function room, it is usually a box with lots of hard surfaces and is very unkind to the sound your equipment will generate. Remember the golden rule with EQ, the less the better. You will have more chance of getting a reasonably good quality sound from your rig than the EQ jockey who rides the treble and bass regardless and only thinks the controls work one way, boost, never cut.

Impedance

Impedance is what you will see quoted on specifications and then the word resistance is used to describe it. Confusing. Well, impedance and resistance are the same thing but occurring in different situations. Resistance is a measurement of an opposing force against a direct current; impedance is a measurement of an opposing force to an alternating current such as an audio signal. Impedance measurement will always be stated as a nominal figure referenced against a stated frequency, because impedance changes with frequency. Although there are impedances quoted for every input and output you can find on the equipment, the most important ones are between amplifiers and speakers.

Impedance is also covered in some detail in Chapter 4 (it is of no use to club DJs, whose only impedance is someone standing in front of them at the bar). To the mobile DJ, an understanding of the forces at work here is an absolute necessity. So we will try to go through it in simple terms. As far as the impedance of mic inputs and amp inputs and headphone outputs, most things should be OK, because the voltage and current levels encountered are not great. That doesn't mean you should not try to match up inputs and outputs, to maintain your gain structure and minimize interference and signal loss.

The current coming out of the amplifier and travelling into the speakers is quite high, in comparison to the signals we have been discussing until now. If, when it travels into the speaker, it does not meet with enough resistance (impedance), the amp will try to send more current than it can produce, it will overheat and give up. Most amplifiers will deliver their rated output, with a respectable signal to noise ratio, into 4 ohms. Some of the better amps will go into 2 ohms, some will even play into a short circuit, 0 ohms and just switch off. The better the amp, the better circuit protection facilities it will have. So that you don't destroy your amp or your speakers, here is how to work out what should be happening.

If two resistances are in line with each other, *in series*, so the output of one feeds into the input of the other, the combined resistance will be the sum total of the two resistances.

Total resistance = R1 + R2

In a parallel circuit, where the source feeds all the resistances simultaneously:

Total resistance = R1 x R2/(R1 + R2)

Total resistance = R1 + R2

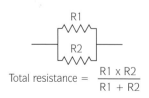
Total resistance = $\frac{R1 \times R2}{R1 + R2}$

Interference

We have already mentioned noise and crosstalk that are, in their basic form, an interference with the sonic purity of the signal. It is also possible to generate interference from without as well as within.

Electric currents generate electro-magnetic interference, which can affect the quality of your signal. For example, if you run lighting cable or mains cable alongside signal cable, your signal cable could pick up a hum from the mains. Interference is one of the reasons why the use of twisted pair shielded cable and balanced lines, to reject interference, are recommended. A ground loop, covered in the safety section, will also cause interference. But one of the commonest problems that could give rise to a hum is caused by inductance, created when a cable with a current running through it is coiled. The simplest way to do this is run your 30-metre extension cable off the drum for 10 metres, leaving 20 metres of it all coiled up and then run 13 amps down it. In doing this you will create an inductive coil, which will in turn create a strong magnetic field, the coil will heat up and so on. In normal circumstances, with for example an electric drill, this isn't critical, although it is not advisable. However, a sound system is going to be on for a lot longer than the 30 seconds it takes to drill a hole and audio signals are quite sensitive to anomalies. The rule is, always uncoil the whole drum, even if you have to pack it in an unruly pile out of the way. Better that than a tight coil round a drum, with current running through it.

The other trip wire for the mobile DJ is, what else is plugged into the same circuit you are using? Wherever possible, avoid the circuit that any coolers or intermittent automatic devices that draw current are also on; anything that is switching on and off on that line, has a potential to interfere with your signal.

Another problem can be RF (radio frequency). Maybe it just so happens that your gig is next door to a taxi office with a fairly high-powered radio transmitter. You end up with all the taxi calls going out through your speakers. Rare nowadays, but it does happen.

Mixing and how it's done

1 The mechanics of the mix

There is no doubt that it seems to be easier to mix for continuous play using vinyl rather than CD. Why this should be I'm quite not sure, but it is so. Would this be the case if the DJ had only ever used CDs? Who knows? All the DJs I've spoken to certainly find it easier to get the mix in using vinyl. So let's take a quick look at the mix, the different types of mix and the way to achieve them.

In the days before varispeed turntables, the simplest mix was the chop mix, one tune stopped the instant another started, or the same one started again and went on a bit longer. To achieve this mix, the two different records needed an almost identical riff between which to chop; an early example is the 12 inch version of 'Ladies' Night' by Kool & The Gang, and 'You Can Do It' by Al Hudson. I went into the mid break on 'Ladies' Night', came out of the start break on 'You Can Do It', no faders, no kill switch, chopped across, one volume down the other up full; hold the record up on a slip mat so it wouldn't slow the turntable down and then let it go.

If you had two records with exactly the same tempo, you could manage a fade across, but this was difficult since there weren't separate tone controls on each channel, just separate rotary volume controls, so you either got it right or you had too much bass or no volume. Then a new turntable arrived on the scene, the Technics SL1200, with a little rotary knob so you could slow a record down or speed it up, but it was for hi fi, not for DJs. In those days, there were usually musicians playing on a record, so the record would start off great, then slow down as the drummer got tired; then speed up again towards the end as the drummer rushed to finish and get to the pub. That made mixing quite difficult, because if you set up the speeds for a beat mix at the start of the track, by the time you got to the break you would have to set the mix up again.

In the space of three years, between 1979 and 1982, everything changed. The Technics SL1200 MKII was born, drum machines like the Roland TR505, 606, 626, 707, 727, 808, 909 and TB303 bass line appeared on dance records, and DJ mixers like the Citronic SM400 finally proved that sound quality and control were an issue that DJs needed to address. As they say, the rest is history. I think it was in 1979 that I put the first commercially available Citronic SM400 into a nightclub in Bredbury near Stockport. 'Disco' had come of age.

The Americans had been the first to start mixing, clubbing was new to them in the 70s, they didn't have *DJs* who could talk, so it was logical that the music should be mixed for continuous dance and it was. In the early 80s, we followed suit.

The Roland TB303 Bassline £80 in 1982, £600 now.

The Roland TR606 Drumatix.

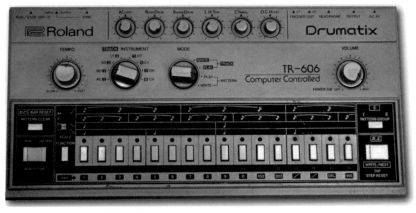

It was still pretty difficult because drum machines were not the norm, so tempos changed, but you learned to cope.

Main types of mixing

Chop mix. Letting one record go at full volume, at a point in time, whilst stopping the one that's playing at the same time as the replacement starts.

Beat mix. Getting two records with a similar sound, matching the beats and then bringing the new one up under the existing one, whilst bringing the volume and bass down on the existing one, so the drum and bass line on the one coming in replaces the one going out. This is the main and most basic type of mix used.

Phrase mix. Coordinating a particular phrase in one record with a near matching one in another, then depending on the tempo and feel of the new record, either doing a chop mix as above or a beat mix.

Shadow or echo mix. Playing the same record on two turntables but having one playing with a delay, so it gives an echo effect. This only works with certain records or portions of them. In this case the bass and volume on the incoming record are reduced, so as not to swamp the original you are trying to echo.

Phase mix. Again, playing the same record on two turntables, but this time at the same speed and in the same time so they are perfectly synced (good way of checking the quartz lock on the turntables). Then delay one very slightly by brushing the edge of the turntable with the back of your hand, this results in a nice whooshing sound around the room when you bring the volume up, with the bass turned down. Modern mixers with effects unit will usually have a phase or flange effect built into them.

Melody mix. This requires the ability to count bars, not just beats, again the beat pattern of the two records needs to be the same; but in this mix, the mix either finishes on a pure melody line over an incoming beat, or starts with a pure melody line over an outgoing beat.

Running mix (break mixing). This is any one or combination of the above, where you use only a portion of an incoming tune, before returning to the previous track being played, then going into a new track. Cross faders can be handy here.

Proxy mix. This used to be T Connection 'Do What You Wanna' or 'At Midnight' years ago. It is a way of mixing two incompatible tunes by using a third record to switch the beats.

Scratch mix. This is where the cross fader comes in handy. It is a version of the original chop mix, where the record is let go, volume raised and then the record is spun back with volume either up or down, (scratching sound).

Mixing with vinyl

Above, if you like, is a directory of the mix. OK, how is it actually done? Well, beat mixing is the starting point, so let's break this down into easy-to-follow steps. Vinyl first.

We are assuming that you have two good quality direct drive turntables and a mixer hooked through an amplifier and speakers. Also that you are able to monitor PFL (pre fader listening) through cans (headphones), on each channel separately and combined. You have balanced your turntable arms, set the anti skate and inserted a slip mat, either on top of the rubber turntable mat or you have taken the rubber mat off and the slip mat is on the metal platter. You have set your gain structure and a record is playing.

The first thing you will need is the next record, which needs to be roughly the same tempo and the same feel as the one already playing.

With the appropriate channel fader turned down, place the next record on the empty turntable, gently lowering the stylus somewhere in the middle of the record, so you can set your trim control (gain structure) on that channel to the correct level on the VU.

With your trim set, you now adjust the EQ on the channel with the track you are introducing (using the record that's playing out as a guide), flicking the PFL in your cans between the sound that's playing and the one you are going to mix into. At the same time, you make sure there isn't too much treble or bass, checking that the gain structure is still OK (remember, the best mix is only noticed after it has happened).

Get your mix records on the turntables.

Gently lower the stylus in the middle of the incoming record…

so you can set the trim control to the correct level.

Adjust the EQ for the incoming record…

then tempo test it by stopping it on the beat then releasing it on the passing beat from the other turntable.

As you are doing all this, you are tempo testing by stopping the incoming record on the beat, holding it on the slip mat and letting it go on the passing beat from the other turntable. Also you are listening to both channels through your cans and adjusting your varispeed control accordingly, to get the tracks nearly to match. (Remember, unless you are using a CD player with a 'Master Tempo' control, altering a record's playing speed also alters its pitch; as the record plays faster, the pitch becomes higher, playing it more slowly will lower the pitch.)

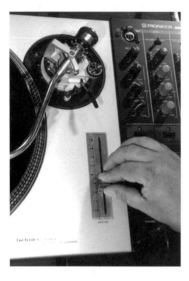

Adjust the varispeed to match beats.

You are now reasonably happy with the set up, so you will set the stylus at the portion of the record you are bringing in, where you intend the mix to start. This could be at the beginning, at a break, wherever.

As the incoming record is playing, you stop it on the slip mat at a main beat, sliding it back (whilst listening in the cans) to the start of the beat. You will need to swing the record backwards and forwards a couple of times to ensure you are on the spot. You will then combine the monitor signal from the channel playing with the one that is cued. As the record you are playing out (and need to mix into) flies past you, let your record go on the beat of the one playing out. Now we arrive at the first controversy. Some DJs like to do this with one ear in the cans and one in the room; the ear in the cans is listening to the record about to come in, the ear in the room is listening to what is being played out. Other DJs do it entirely in the cans, either one turntable in one side, one in the other (if the facility exists on the mixer), or both turntables mixed in both cans. You will have to find the method that works best for you.

Place the stylus where you want the mix to start.

Swing the record back and forth a bit to find the right spot.

This is where the mix is made, you have to get the beats to match, either by speeding up or slowing down the incoming track using the varispeed control. Or, if the tempo is right but not quite on the beat of the track playing out, you can vary the turntable speed very slightly. Slow it down for a fraction, by putting your hand on the side of it, or speed it up by spinning the centre of the record slightly faster on the slip mat.

Slow it down... or speed it up by hand to get the beats to match.

So now the beats match, you may be ready to go straight into the mix, or not, in which case reposition the needle on the record coming in and re cue it. Now you know that the beats match, you may need to repeat the process above slowing down or speeding up the turntable. Now for the mix.

You have combined the monitor signals in the can, you let your track go on the beat of the one playing out and are able to hear both records, the tempos match. Now bring up the fader on the incoming track, to increase its volume whilst reducing the bass EQ control on the track playing out. Bass is where volume lives, so while you are bringing up the volume on one side and reducing the bass on the other, you are effectively substituting bass lines without affecting the gain structure. When the fader on the incoming track reaches the top, the fader on the other side should be brought down, or left if you are still using the melody, even though the bass has already gone. That's the mix in, done, gone.

Bring up the fader on the incoming track and reduce the bass on the other.

The whole procedure, when you know your records and you have practised, will take 30 seconds. Certainly the last step, although it may seem long, can be done virtually as a chop mix or over 2–3 seconds.

If you do this and get a boom, bang result instead of a boom, boom result, you have mixed on the wrong beat that's all; more on that later. Now let's repeat this process using CDs.

Mixing with CDs

We are assuming here that you have two good CD players and a mixer hooked through an amplifier and speakers. Also that you are able to monitor PFL through cans. You have set your gain structure and a track is playing.

With the appropriate channel fader down, you place the next CD into the empty CD player, skipping to the middle of the track you want to play so you can set your trim control (gain structure) to the correct level on the VU.

Place the incoming CD into the player.

Skip to the middle of the track and set trim.

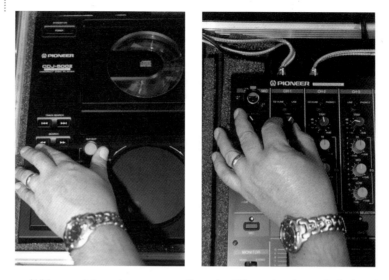

With your trim set, you now adjust the EQ on the channel playing the track you are introducing, using the record that's playing out as a guide and flicking the PFL in your cans between the one that's playing and the one you are going to mix into. Make sure that there isn't too much treble or bass and keep an ever-watchful eye on that gain structure. (CDs are pretty similar when it comes to tone and volume control, they don't seem to have the variances that are found in vinyl).

Adjust EQ to suit.

As you can't physically hold the CD, the little tests you do at this stage are slightly different than with vinyl. You need to hit Pause, on the beat, use the jog wheel to take you back to the start of the beat and then hit Play as the track playing out goes past on the beat. The trouble is, when you Pause a CD player, you put it into a tiny loop, which continually plays in Pause mode, until you press Play again. To repeat the process you have to Pause, Reset and Play again. To get round this the simplest thing to do is to set a new cue point, to where the playing head will return whenever you press Cue. So you repeat the little sequence above, finding the beat, pausing the CD, jogging back to the start of the beat, rocking the jog wheel over the start to make sure you are in the right place, then you press Cue. That is now your cue point for that track and, what's more, that little loop that was playing while the machine was in Pause mode has gone (the re-cue procedure may differ slightly between makes of CD players). Whilst listening to both channels through your cans and adjusting your varispeed control accordingly, you get the tracks to match, then you rehearse the beat matching, using the Start button, as the beat goes past on the track playing out. Use the varispeed control to bring the incoming track to the speed of the track playing out, (with the 'Master Tempo' con-

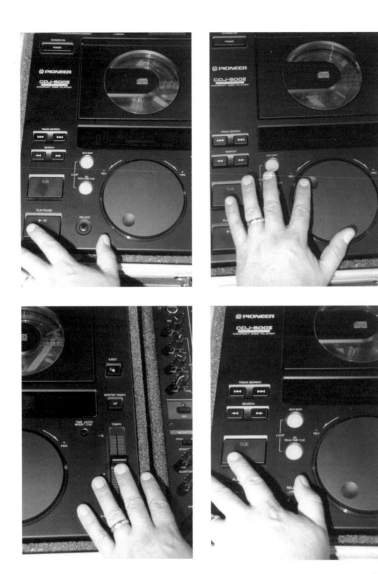

Hit Pause, on the beat...

then use the jog wheel to take you back to the start of the beat.

Adjust varispeed to match beats then hit Cue.

To start rehearsal again just press Cue.

trol engaged, altering the speed of the playing track does not alter its pitch). To start a rehearsal again, all you do is press Cue and then start on the beat.

You are now happy with the set up, so you will go to your cue point at the beginning of the incoming track, at a break, wherever.

As the track playing out goes past you, press the start button on the incoming track on the beat of the one playing out, whilst listening to both channels through your cans. As with vinyl, some DJs like to do this with one ear in the cans and one in the room, again you will have to find the method that works for you.

This is where the mix is made. You may have to repeat some portions above, just teasing the jog wheel to get the perfect match, but from now on, what works for vinyl also works for CDs.

You are able to hear both tracks, the tempos match. Now bring up the fader on the incoming track to increase its volume, whilst reducing the bass EQ control on the track playing out. Bass is where volume lives, so while you are bringing up the

Tease the jog wheel to get the perfect match.

Tip

When using CD controls, keep your fingers on the buttons and press. Don't hover above the buttons and then move your hand or finger down. The split second it takes for your finger to reach the button is enough to mess up your timing. CDs have an instant, instant start, there is no lead in at all. Also, the control switches are likely to fail if hit continuously rather than pressed.

volume on one side and reducing the bass on the other, you are effectively substituting bass lines and not affecting the gain structure. When the incoming fader reaches the top, the fader on the other side should be brought down, even though the bass has already gone. That's the mix is in, done, gone.

Compared with vinyl, the time scale is slightly longer, say 40 seconds, but with some CD players you can re-cue, re-loop, use fader and/or cross fader, start and re-cue, the creative possibilities are endless. If you are fortunate enough to get to play with a set of these and have a good sense of rhythm, you will be truly astounded at what you can do.

Bring up the fader in the incoming track whilst reducing the bass EQ on the track playing out.

Tip

A good way to get a mix set up on CD is by using the loop function. Put a continuous and even loop into the track you are about to mix in and line that up with the track playing out. When you are ready, just bring up the volume on the loop coming in, whilst losing the bass on the track going out, once the mix is in let the loop go.

Again, if you get boom, bang instead of boom, boom you have mixed on the wrong beat. You need to know how to count, where bars are and where beats are within a bar.

Counting

How to explain how to count? Each piece of music has a time signature, i.e. how many beats make up one bar. A beat is a basic (rhythmic) unit in a piece of music, and they are usually grouped in twos, threes or fours. Modern dance music is in 4/4 time, 4 beats in each bar. If you were reading a dance music score it would tell you 4/4 (the time signature) and the drum part in that score would show 4 beats in that bar. The rhythm is determined by where the accent falls. A samba is 4/4 time, so is reggae, rock and bhangra, yet they all have varying rhythm patterns depending on where the accents fall in a bar.

Basic 4/4 time is *boom, bang, boom, bang*, next bar and so on. Boom is the kick or bass drum, bang is the snare drum. For good mixing, you need not only to be able to match rhythm patterns and sounds, but to be able to count bars. I could show you how to count bars but I can't tell you, I just know where they are. As you are playing a track count 1, 2, 3, 4 on the beats. The heaviest kick or bass drumbeat will usually be on the first beat in the bar, which is also where a verse may start or a crescendo peak. After you have been listening to music for a while, it will come naturally, so don't be unduly concerned if at first you get the tempo right but mix in the wrong place.

You will notice I don't mention the cross fader in this mechanics section. In a digital world where you can set and reset CD Cue points automatically using them, their importance as a creative tool, becomes obvious. What we have here are the basics if you can learn these, you can then add something extra that you are comfortable with, that works for you. That may well be the cross fader. I know scratch DJs use cross faders extensively, I have never learnt to scratch. Added to that, I learnt to mix in the pre-cross fader days on a Formula Sound mixer, where you had to bring up one fader, whilst bringing the bass down on the other channel. I still think this method allows you more control and it is easier to escape if the mix is going pear shaped.

Without wishing to put anyone down, it has to be said that mixing is more practice than talent. Having said that, some people will take to it more easily than others, but basic mixing certainly is a skill acquired by practice. It helps if you have a good ear and a good memory but practice is the key. Most 12 inch dance records made today are designed to be 'mix' friendly, that way the record gets played. So it's a question of creative combining rather than raw talent. Unless you can find a club to practise in, you will need understanding parents, neighbours or flat mates, because two hours a day of that dull bass thud is usually more than people can stand.

What about just using headphones? Well, something is lacking if you are just using cans, the sound has got to get out into the room, only then will you have a true appreciation of maintaining the levels and bass content (gain structure) whilst mixing at the same time. If you get onto a 5kW rig you can't have the levels all

Tip

With very rare exceptions, the rule is, the bass line of the incoming record takes the place of that of the outgoing record. So it's fader going up and bass set on the incoming record, bass down on the outgoing record as the fader comes up on the incoming record, then fader down on the outgoing record.

over the place. The headphones are where you rehearse the mix before you play it out, but you must play it out for completion.

If you are going to practise in a bedroom, you don't need a 500 watt amp and a pair of 300 watt speakers. A small amp and good hi fi or monitor speakers will do. Control your levels, that is the key, the mix should be seamless and only noticeable after the event, not whilst it is happening. As the sound gets louder, any differences become more noticeable. What may sound perfect in the cans can be all over the place in the room, similarly when the transition is made from a small PA to a large one.

Everyone develops a slightly different technique, it's a question of whatever works for you, feels good and keeps the crowd happy. The nicest thing about mixing is that a new track can be introduced to the crowd without firstly asking their permission. It just happens, it's in the mix. In days gone by, in the era of 'that was' and 'this is' introductions, often the floor would empty, irrespective of the quality of a particular record, if the crowd didn't recognize the introductory name. In fact some unscrupulous DJs would lie about what was coming on next just to keep the floor full.

2 In the mix (mixing beats and bars, counting time)

The preceding part of this chapter deals with the mechanics of the mix, how it's done, how and why certain things need to be set up certain ways, gain structures etc., the physical elements. But since Djing is about the music, let's take a less logical and mechanical journey, and try to understand the organic process involved.

For the sake of argument all the music we will deal with will be deemed to be in 4/4 time. 4/4 means 4 beats in a bar. Now I am not a musician so apologies in advance to those of you that know music, and keys, and chords and that kind of stuff I am assuming that we who are trying to grasp what follows are not musicians.

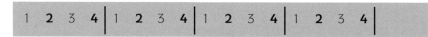

The above is a visual representation of the beats in 4 bars, most things happen after even numbered spaces 2, 4 or 8 bars, indeed the instrumental break in the middle of older records was referred to as the middle 8.

Since all 4/4 records conform to the above you could be forgiven for thinking that all 4/4 records will join together seamlessly. Well of course we know they don't, one of the main factors is tempo, or how fast the beats occur in a given recording. A tempo of 122 BPM (beats per minute) will not seamlessly mix with a record with a tempo of 139 BPM, or indeed with one of 124 BPM, that where the vari-speed controls on turntables and CD's come in. The other obstacle to 'like mixing with like' is rhythm, or what is played around those four beats and where. This is crucial because funk, samba, house, garage, hardcore, r & b, hip-hop, rap and reggae are all ostensively in 4/4 time.

Another thing not to assume when looking at the drawing above is that every 'beat' represents a physical drumbeat. It doesn't, a beat is a measure of musical time, you can have 4/4 time, and no drumbeat at all, when the drum strikes on the beat that is known as syncopated.

Syncopation usually occurs on the backbeat (beats 2 and 4 slightly heavier in the drawing) of the musical time. So beat 1, whilst on paper, may not exist as a strike on a drum, but beat 2, the backbeat may exist as both musical time and as a physical drum sound, more common in older records than now.

The best physical way to demonstrate modern beats is to listen to a record that we all know. *Billie Jean* by Michael Jackson is the perfect example which has been endlessly and shamelessly copied by everyone since 1985, although it was not the first record to give more or less equal weight to all the beats it is probably the most well known. It starts on beat 1, then just count:

1	2	3	4	2	2	3	4	3	2	3	4	4	2	3	4

that way you have counted both beats and bars, 1 being the first bar, substituting 2 for 1 in the second bar and so on. If you do this you will find that the record builds, coincide with beats, and after certain numbers of bars. Let's apply the template above to *Billie Jean* and see what happens. B= Bass Drum S= Snare.

1	2	3	4	2	2	3	4	3	2	3	4	4	2	3	4
B	S	B	S	B	S	B	S	B	S	B	S	B	S	B	S

After 2 bars bass line starts 1st beat of third bar.

5	2	3	4	6	2	3	4	7	2	3	4	8	2	3	4

After 6 bars little shaker just before 1st beat of bar seven.

9	2	3	4	10	2	3	4	11	2	3	4	12	2	3	4

After 10 bars a counter point synth starts on beat 1 of bar 11 mimicking the beat duh duh – duh duh. After bar 14 the vocal starts on beat 1 of bar 15.

If all this is so obvious to you, turn the page. If not, I urge you to get *Billie Jean* and count and keep counting. You will soon find you are able to pick out the first beat of a bar anywhere in this, and indeed any record, and soon you will instinctively know when certain things are going to happen. The guitar break in the middle of *Billie Jean* is 8 bars long just like the middle 8 of old, the vocal starts again after bar 9.

I'm using older records as an example because we all know them, so that makes them easy to deal with as examples, but the theory works on any record.

OK we have got *Billie Jean* nailed down let's mix out of it into *Holiday* by Madonna roughly the same tempo slightly slower, so you will need to use your varispeed to speed it up a little, *Holiday* has a different feel, much lighter than the bass and snare heavy *Billie Jean*, let's bar map *Holiday*.

Holiday starts with a low bass drum keeping time, and a bit of a synth playing half time (every second beat) over the top, you have to count through the synth, it's a bit tricky at first. The main synth melody joins after 4 bars at bar 5, the break and drums kick in after bar 8 on bar 9.

1	2	3	4	2	2	3	4	3	2	3	4	4	2	3	4
B	B	B	B	B	B	B	B	B	B	B	B	B	B	B	B

Bass drums keeps time with counterpoint synth in background.

5	2	3	4	6	2	3	4	7	2	3	4	8	2	3	4
B	B	B	B	B	B	B	B	B	B	B	B	B	B	B	B

Main melody synth starts 4th beat bar 4 to bar 5. Main synth melody starts here over bass drum keeping time.

9	2	3	4	10	2	3	4	11	2	3	4	12	2	3	4
B	S	B	S	B	S	B	S	B	S	B	S	B	S	B	S

Break on 4th bar 8 main drums start on the 1st beat of bar 9.

The first vocal in *Holiday* happens on bar 25. So the construction here is slightly different, setting the first two events up on the last (4th) beat of the preceding bar. Once you can count musical beats, you don't actually need them to be there physically to count them, that's where mixing melody lines, or acappellas (which a lot of records give you as a bonus track) from one track, over drum breaks in other tracks becomes a breeze, you know where the first beat of the bar is without it being physically present, and you can count, and tap out the tempo accordingly.

Back to Michael and Madonna, you want to mix out of Billie Jean into *Holiday*. In this scenario I would guess that I want *Holiday* to be in by bar 5 where the melody line kicks off, in readiness for the breaks and drums starting properly.

Billie Jean has an 8 bar 'middle 8' instrumental break so, in theory, I could beat match and drop Holiday in here with 3 bars to spare, but I don't really want to upset the bar structure too much. So if I could get Holiday started on the first bar of the break then I would be in by bar 4, half way through. Or I could start *Holiday* 4 bars before the *Billie Jean* instrumental break so it starts on the break itself making Holiday the intro into *Billie Jean's* middle eight, well nearly. The key is, how that guitar break sounds in *Billie Jean*, do I let it play a little, or do I cut it out in the slight lull before it kicks in, or perhaps get *Holiday* in at the end before the vocal comes back. What do you think?

Now that is an organic, emotional, musical decision, that has nothing to do with anything other than what you think sounds right. I try to get *Holiday* going under the build to the middle 8 of *Billie Jean*, 8 bars in front so the drums from *Billie Jean* carry *Holiday* while the *Holiday* melody plays underneath. *Holiday* kicks in on its own at exactly the time that Michael gets to his hee hee. I find that if the crowd are rocking this keeps them there. 16 bars later the vocal starts it's a nice build up into an 80's retro mix that goes into The Human League, Kool and The Gang, New Order and others.

Nowadays it's easy, the record might as well have a pointer on it saying mix here, or here, or here, or here (I'll expand on this later). But back in the old days you had to figure it out, you had to look for a break in which to slip your mix.

It has to be said that while this is an easy example, because more or less everyone knows both tracks, it is not the easiest of mixes. But if you can get this right then the new stuff shouldn't present any problem whatsoever. Billie Jean is the perfect example of modern syncopated dance music. If you can't bar count then it's a perfect medium to use to learn. Once you can bar count and match tempo, your mixing skills will go though the roof if?

If you remember that different styles of music, whilst written in the same musical time, use different rhythm patterns, and that in combining these, you create the mood and style, and hopefully 'rising excitement', which you need, to build to a crescendo in your set. In other words start of slow and small and finish off faster and big.

Earlier when I said modern records might as well have pointers on them saying mix here or here or here I wasn't kidding. There aren't many modern dance records that don't give at least two or three opportunities to get out of them into another track and, more importantly, a way out using a slightly different rhythm pattern that changes the mood slightly so that you can take the set in a different direction.

This is commercially sound, if you make a good dance record that a DJ can come out of into many different sets, then it's more likely to be played. So a record will break down into a beat, just drums and bass, or just drums, or drums bass and some Latin percussion or down to a melody line with the bass and drums eq'd out so that you can fit something appropriate over the top.

This is where the 'art' of Djing kicks in. Building the set through several different tracks to end up an hour later with a bit of a crescendo. The first thing you need to know about this is that you have to be very good indeed if you are going to mix across genres, because certain patterns or rhythms don't sit very well together, and, usually therefore, appeal to a different fan base. Having said that I've been to gigs where the DJ could have played a Kazoo and still had the crowd eating out of his hand. But generally stick within a style and tempo range, say tempo's of between 122BPM and 130BPM then 130BPM to 139BPM.

For my Club set, which I imaginatively called 'Smooth N' Heavy', I play straight 122BPM to 128 maybe 130BPM tempo tracks, I favour vocal tracks, (my beginnings with soul music) I like to have a Latin and or Jazz feel in there, so I look for percussive pieces with a heavy bass and drum line, with hooks, and counterpoint rhythm guitar, and high register synth and strings. I find that these records allow me access to over 20 years of tracks that will slide together nicely. Even mixing originals back into their 21st Century loop sampled successors. Where possible, I will start the set down at the 122BPM end and build it up as I go along, to finish at 128BPM. The Latin feel stuff comes in at the higher BPM range. That's me, that's what I am comfortable with. Richard Hibbert a Hard House specialist from Leeds starts hard and heavy at about 133BPM for a smooch, and off he goes. I played a set before him once, to his crowd, and they were nearly asleep.

Rhythm patterns

Rhythm patterns and bass sounds are tremendously important, it's no accident that drums are used to work a crowd up into frenzy, it's the way we are programmed, drums and bass are exciting. Music is after all a combination of musical elements to generate a feeling, an emotional response.

In the past, this was/is done solely with percussion that played both high and low sounds. As we became more 'cultured' we lost percussion, certainly rhythmic percussion, in favour of sweeping strings and French horns and things. Then we looked back to older cultures who borrowed modern instruments to evolve their music and realised that there were enjoying it much more than we were even when they were singing about the saddest things (The Blues) but more importantly the music they played had a 'beat' and what a beat. I defy anyone to listen to Rag Time Jazz, Billie Holiday or an artist like John Lee Hooker without tapping their feet. The pattern of Blues is 4/4, with some artistic license and the rhythm is solid even without bass and drums because these musicians understand at an instinctive level the importance of musical timing, and how to fit around a beat. Funk is generally defined as being late on beats one and three, (our ears can detect milliseconds of delay) listen to James Brown to see the effect that musical timing has on the sound he generates, and in turn the emotional response that generates.

Some clever person said, time is the only thing we have, it's what we do with it that counts. This statement is never truer than in music, we have 4 beats (measures of musical time in a bar) it's what the musicians do with it, around it, and in relation to it that counts. That's what gives us different styles/genres of music.

The key to being a good mixer, is knowing the music you're playing, being able to count beats and bars, knowing how and where to fit certain tracks together, understanding gain structure and the effect it has on what you play out, looking at the crowd and anticipating their desires. It will take longer than 5 minutes to learn, and master, and it is all about the music.

Once you can bar count, even simple chop mixes seem to flow better, rather than just letting a record start as another one fades out you will find yourself going 1, 2, 3, 4 on the fade and then hitting the start button to coincide with beat 1 of the next bar, because that's where you've set the cue point.

I could waffle on for pages giving examples of different rhythm structures but all you really need to know is, if it sounds good use it, you will find some magical combinations.

One word of warning and advice I would offer, is that once you master the mix, some DJ's can become mix happy, chopping and changing, showing off their skills as mixers. I would always say let the music do the work, unless of course that's what your crowd want. Usually you need to give people time to get into the groove, sounds corny, but music is about emotional response and a little time in the groove is needed to maximise that response.

The mobile DJ

Carting it about

The club DJ only has to cart around a heavy record box or two, he probably couldn't even lift a speaker (only kidding). The mobile DJ on the other hand has to carry around, deliver and set up a full sound and lighting system. So let's take a quick look at some things that might help him.

Find someone else to do the carrying. This is a good idea, if you can afford it. Get someone to carry the gear and set it up. This could be a friend, a relative or just someone taking advice from this book and attaching themselves to you to learn how it is all done. Welcome them with open arms. They carry it in, they set it up and you wire it up. As the relationship progresses, they wire up and maybe even start the night off for you. Their path (obviously) is, eventually, to do what you do. They are getting paid whilst training and you are getting help, especially at the end of the night when you really need it.

Get a bigger van than you actually need, rather than cramming everything in. Organize your van so that you have room to reach things, without unloading other things. Make sure the van has an alarm and an immobilizer and that it's a proper one, that works on all doors and windows. Never signwrite your van, unless you have a secure off road parking area. All rear windows should be blanked out (bars and mirrored inserts are good).

The mobile DJ's equipment lives in the van. If there are any doubts about the security of the vehicle, the items that are hard to replace, easy to steal or easy to sell should be removed. CD players and CDs are the main ones, no opportunist thief is going to run down the road carrying a 30 kilo speaker or a rack case weighing 25 kilos. Make sure that your alarm is one that will not be ignored, it helps, but also make sure your equipment is marked with your details and that the marking is large and distinctive.

Make sure you have a trolley and/or a sack truck, avoid gigs with too many steps, which is why it is advisable to recce a venue before agreeing to do a job. Observe the correct position when lifting anything heavy, back straight, legs bent etc., think about what you are doing and take your time. Use the sack truck and trolley, and don't do any more carting by hand than is absolutely necessary. Allow sufficient time to get to the venue and set up before you start, when you are rushing you have accidents.

Water and electricity are not good relations, if your equipment gets wet, that will not necessarily destroy it on its own. Only when you plug it in and switch it on (while it is still wet) will that happen. If your equipment does get wet, let it dry out completely before attempting to use it again. Never load or unload unprotected electrical equipment in the rain, cover it up. If it gets wet, do not use it.

Tip

Always set and wire up with MAINS UNPLUGGED.

Setting up, wiring and troubleshooting

Typical wiring setup basic rigs

Balanced lines should be used wherever the equipment allows. The use of twisted pair shielded cable is recommended, whether shop bought or made to order. If you have to use unbalanced leads, use high grade, low capacitance shielded wire to get the best results. For connecting a balanced output to an unbalanced input, the pseudo-balanced configuration may help eliminate any potential hum problems (see figure on page 42).

Always use good quality, oxygen free copper leads and never use the little thin phono leads that are often supplied. Make sure you follow the right/left convention, it makes life a lot easier if you develop a fault.

Connector Wiring Standards (B) typically balanced (UB) unbalanced (D) digital

- (B) The 3 pin XLR (which is also used as an AES/EBU digital connection).
- (UB) 6.35mm mono phone Jack.
- (B or UB) 6.35mm mono/stereo phone Jack.
- (UB)(D) RCA phono connector (also used as a SPDIF digital connection (75 ohm impedance) and video connection), usually found between turntable or CD player and mixer.
- (D) TOSlink or optical: used to interconnect digital equipment to keep signal in the digital domain.
- (UB) Neutrik Speakon Connector usually found between amplifier and speaker.

Tip

PC (see Chapter 14) are a good source of leads, cables and connectors at reasonable prices.

These are the most common connectors you will come across and they will give you the most trouble. There are a host of others with which you should become familiar but at this stage you need only concern yourself with the above.

Figure 7.03 shows the wiring convention, now standard in 17 countries, for the above connectors. Any equipment still using pin 3 as positive/hot on XLRs is not conforming to the current standard.

Plug turntables into RIAA/phono inputs or the channel input and select phono not line. Plug CD players into line inputs or the channel input and select line not phono. Ensure that the output from your mixer is compatible with the input to your graphic and the output from your graphic is compatible with the input to your amp. If there are variable settings, they are usually at +4dBu or −10dBV, in reality this means high line or medium line settings, you need to match these up. If you are unsure of what level a particular piece of equipment uses, consult the manual. If there isn't one, assume that the level is −10dBV. If you do insert an Aural Exciter® into the signal chain, make sure the ins and outs are set to be compatible too.

Ensure that the amplifier is the correct rating for the speakers and vice versa. Overdriving the speakers will destroy them, underdriving can affect sound quality.

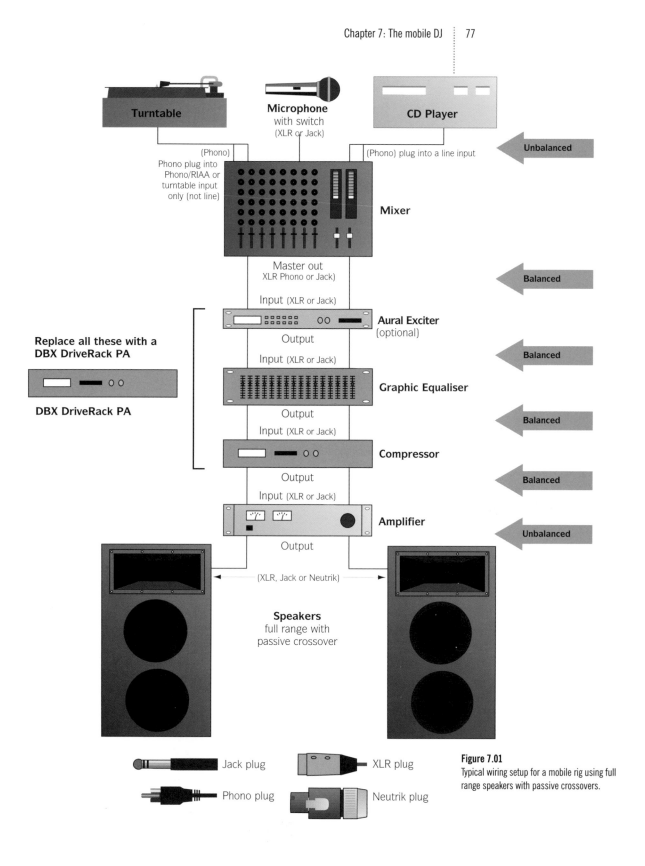

Turntable

Microphone
with switch
(XLR or Jack)

CD Player

Unbalanced

(Phono)
Phono plug into
Phono/RIAA or
turntable input
only (not line)

(Phono) plug into a line input

Mixer

Master out
XLR Phono or Jack)

Input (XLR or Jack)

Balanced

**Replace all these with a
DBX DriveRack PA**

DBX DriveRack PA

Aural Exciter
(optional)

Output

Input (XLR or Jack)

Balanced

Graphic Equaliser

Output

Input (XLR or Jack)

Balanced

Compressor

Output

Input (XLR or Jack)

Balanced

Amplifier

Unbalanced

Output

(XLR, Jack or Neutrik)

Speakers
full range with
passive crossover

Jack plug

XLR plug

Phono plug

Neutrik plug

Figure 7.01
Typical wiring setup for a mobile rig using full
range speakers with passive crossovers.

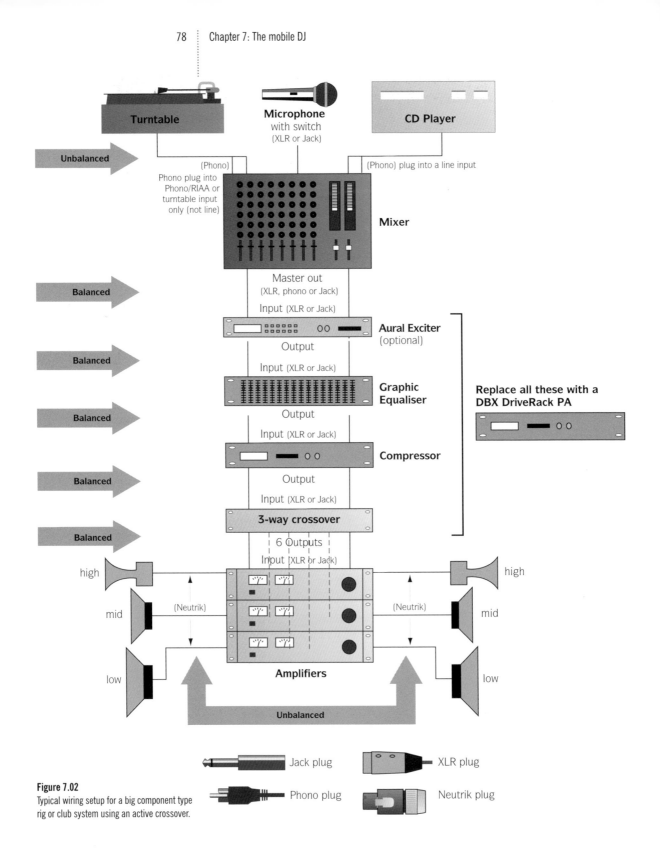

Turntable

Microphone
with switch
(XLR or Jack)

CD Player

Unbalanced

(Phono)
Phono plug into
Phono/RIAA or
turntable input
only (not line)

(Phono) plug into a line input

Mixer

Master out
(XLR, phono or Jack)

Input (XLR or Jack)

Balanced

Aural Exciter
(optional)

Output

Input (XLR or Jack)

Balanced

**Graphic
Equaliser**

Replace all these with a
DBX DriveRack PA

Output

Input (XLR or Jack)

Balanced

Compressor

Output

Input (XLR or Jack)

Balanced

3-way crossover

6 Outputs

Input (XLR or Jack)

Balanced

high

high

(Neutrik)

(Neutrik)

mid

mid

Amplifiers

low

low

Unbalanced

Jack plug

XLR plug

Phono plug

Neutrik plug

Figure 7.02
Typical wiring setup for a big component type
rig or club system using an active crossover.

Balanced and unbalanced connector wiring standards

3 pin XLR	6.35 mm TRS Phono	Standard wiring convention (balanced)
Pin 1	Sleeve	ground/shield (earth, screen)
Pin 2	Tip	positive (signal, high, hot)
Pin 3	Ring	negative (signal reference, return, low, common)

6.35 mm TRS Phono	Phono (RCA)	Standard wiring convention (unbalanced)
Tip	Centre pin	positive (signal)
Sleeve	Outer	ground/shield (and signal reference/return)

Once you have wired everything up, ensure that everything is switched off before you plug the mains in, then switch on the power. Once the mains are on, switch on the equipment in this order:

1   Turntables/CD players.
2   Mixer.
3   Graphic.
4   Amplifier with volumes turned down.
    (Always switch the amplifiers on last with the volumes down. Leave everything for 30 seconds or so to warm up.) Then:
5   Flatten the EQ.
6   Set the gain structure of the mixer.
7   Follow the gain structure through the graphic.
8   Gently turn up the volume on the left side of the amp, check for output then turn it down.
9   Gently turn up the volume on the right side of the amp, check for output and turn it down.
10 Assuming you have a sound from both sides of your system, everything is OK so far.
11 Turn both sides of the amplifier to a nice, low, gentle level to allow current to flow, have a walk into the room and start setting the EQ.

Info

Beware of condensation, if it's been cold in your van and you are now in a warm room, when you first set up don't switch on straight away, give the equipment time to warm up naturally.

One of the differences between live sound and a mobile DJ, is in the area of controlling the final volume. In a live sound situation, the amplifiers are very often in a remote location, away from the sound desk. So what the engineers do is follow the switching-on sequence as above, crank the amps up to full and set the subsequent levels at the desk. The mobile DJ doesn't do that. He can; but my advice is to stick to getting the gain structure right at the mixer and the component devices that follow it; then get the levels in the room out from the amplifier, by adjusting the volume controls accordingly.

Once the gain structure is set, that is it, there is no more volume to be had from the mixer, without the danger of distortion. So from then on make the adjustments at the amp. The mobile DJ is close enough to reach the amp, the situation is not the same as in live sound, where the amps and speakers can be remotely situated or inaccessible to the musicians. So the advice is, take advantage of the situation and the extra control this gives you, to preserve and lengthen the life of speakers and amplifiers, by only turning the amp up as high as is needed at the time.

My reasons for this advice are mainly quality based, but another thing that has to be remembered is that there are very few live sound situations where a band plays for 4–5 hours continuously. A mobile DJ will regularly do a 4-hour stint. Why have the amp flat out for all that time if you don't have to? Your equipment is going to last longer if it is not on the edge of its performance envelope for long periods of time.

Switching off is always in this order:

1   Amplifier volume down.
2   Amplifier off then back through the chain.

Always turn down the volume and switch the amplifier off first, before switching anything else off.

Troubleshooting

Always pursue a calm and logical course if you come across a problem. If there is a burbling sound coming from one of the speakers, this usually indicates that something, somewhere in that channel's signal chain is shorting out. First, unplug the speaker and try it on the other side of the amp, assuming that side is OK. If the speaker still sounds bad, the chances are that either the crossover or the speaker has blown. If the speaker sounds good, plug the speaker back into the bad side, then go back through the signal chain, swapping leads from the good side to the bad, starting with the speaker lead, until by a process of elimination the problem is isolated. The reason you use the leads from the other side of the stereo system is because if the other side is good, the leads are good, so proven components are being used to detect the fault. Do not use another lead that is not currently in use, it may also be faulty.

More often than not, the problem will be due to a loose lead or broken plug. It has to be said that today's electronics are very reliable unless abused. If the fault is with a component in the channel, providing it is not the amplifier or the mixer, it can usually be removed and everything can carry on with just the sacrifice of a little quality.

If one side of the mixer has gone down, go to mono and play the good side out into both sides of the equipment chain that follows. Similarly with the graphic, go to mono, unplug the bad side and carry on, or stay in stereo and do without the graphic for one night.

If one channel of the amp has gone down, go to mono and play on through the good side. Providing you are within the impedance range of the amplifier, you can move the affected channel's speakers onto the mono channel, all that will be lost is stereo imaging.

If, when everything is switched on and there is power to everything and there is an output from the mixer but there is no sound at all, from one side or both, this usually indicates a plug not fully inserted. Everybody has done this and then spent a panicky few minutes thrashing around trying to find the catastrophic failure that doesn't exist. Remember, proceed logically.

A very good reason not to whack up the volume when you first switch on is because now, as you retrace your steps, checking that every plug is properly inserted, when you come across the culprit you will immediately have sound – at the level you have set. A lower level is better for your system and for any people who may also be in the room. If there is definitely no loose lead, the next most likely culprit is a blown fuse. Fuses are like small light bulbs, in as much as they usually fail when switched on or off. There is no way that you can predict when this is likely to happen. You must carry spare fuses, for all your equipment. The financial cost is pennies. Next, you need to determine how far through the signal chain the signal is going, unless of course there is an obvious indication of where the fault lies i.e. mains light not illuminated on a unit, or lack of signal indicator activity on a unit.

The nice thing about stereo is that if you do have an equipment failure, it is usually on one side or the other, so switching to mono is a short-term remedy until you can get the unit replaced or repaired. In the case of amplifiers, if there is a power supply problem and both sides of the amp rely on a common power supply, then the amp is out. That is why the best advice is to carry a spare amp. Also, the amplifier is the workhorse of the system, if any component is likely fail it will be the amp, it does the most work, generates the most heat and is dealing with the most current.

There are various other maladies than can affect equipment but these usually occur when the system is initially set up, or when new components are introduced. Things like leads being incorrectly wired, causing phase cancellation problems, or short circuits. There may be incompatibilities through the signal chain, which can cause a loss of volume. Usually these, once rectified, will not occur again.

The general rule of thumb is that the better you treat your equipment, the better it will work for you. Faults and failures are bound to occur but rough or inappropriate handling will increase their likelihood. Look after your gear and it will look after you. Then, when you are ready to upgrade, you will get more for it.

Mobile DJ/club sound vs. live sound

The dynamics of playing a music recording are very different from those of playing live music. The dynamics of a live show are entirely controllable from a sound engineering point of view. An engineer controls the amounts of compression, EQ, or effects used, in real time. With a recording, all these dynamics already exist, although the DJ may add further dynamic processing.

Most recordings are not made with the intention that they sound good on a massive PA system. They are made to sound good on a home hi fi or car stereo. This is why, in every recording studio, the final mix down is usually played back on a pair of Yamaha NS10s, which are basically small hi fi type speakers. Now, with the introduction of CD, DVD, Dolby surround sound and active speaker systems with subwoofers, things are changing slightly. Although recordings are now the best quality that they have ever been, they are also the most dynamically manipulated.

One of the reasons for trying to use as little additional EQ and dynamics when playing back a recording is because of the amount of dynamics already present in the recording.

Years ago, I heard a track on the radio and thought, 'that's good, I'll buy it'. I did, but when I listened to it at home on my CD player, it sounded nothing like the track I remembered from the radio. This was due to dynamic processing. To get a punchier sound, the radio station's output was fed through a compressor. This altered the dynamics of the sound of this particular track so much, as to more or less create a different track.

Whereas PA systems are used to play both commercial recordings and live sound, the two outputs are similar but not identical. There is a subtle difference between the dynamics of the two disciplines, which needs to be understood and acknowledged. Good music playback speakers do not necessarily make good PA speakers and vice versa. In a small PA system, a pair of expensive speakers on stands may make a band sound great, but equally they can make a music playback system sound bad. They may be good PA speakers, suitable for sound reinforcement applications, but that doesn't necessarily make them good playback speakers.

To date (and I am open to correction here), the only off-the-shelf speakers I have found that can actually be switched between 'playback' and 'vocal', are Cerwin Vegas and RCFs. (No doubt I will get some voluble letters telling me about a lot more.) I have also found that whilst there are some excellent speaker chassis available, ready made shop sold cabinets which feature these units are mostly designed for catch all work, not DJ work.

There are specialist installation companies, whose speaker products are dance club oriented, but their product never seems to reach the mobile DJ, unless of course, it's in a dance tent at a festival, or at a promoted venue.

This is a very important consideration that is mostly overlooked by PA and sound reinforcement engineers. The mobile DJ is still considered to be a poor relation, not demanding much skill. This is somewhat annoying when the opposite is true, he/she really is a multi skilled individual.

So when you are out and about, listening to live music played by musicians and wondering why music that's pre-recorded doesn't sound as clean and vibrant as the live stuff, it's all to do with the different dynamics involved in amplifying a sound. It is one of the reasons that live sound is so good

Hazard awareness, health and safety

8

Perhaps at first glance there doesn't seem to be anything particularly dangerous about being a DJ, but danger lurks in the most unlikely places. In addition to your own safety, as the DJ you have to be aware of the safety of many other people, who are mostly your employer's customers. Safety has many different facets for the DJ.

Your awareness and professionalism could save you, or a member of the public from injury. You, as the DJ, the person "in charge", need to be aware of all the potential hazards of your profession, from wet fire escape steps, to trailing wires and much more. Every area of what you do needs to objectively assessed for the hazards created, for both you, and the public, failure to do so, and failure to make safe or give clear warning of hazards to others, could leave you liable for any damage or injury to a third party.

Hazards for the DJ

No matter how innocuous being a DJ might seem, a DJ uses electricity and electricity has the capability to kill. The worst thing about electricity is, it's undetectable, you can't see, smell, or feel it until it's too late. Remember that it is ever present.

Most club installations are pretty well kept and maintained, if you have any doubts, a quick check with a multimeter will allay any fears. The things to check are all metal surfaces that are close to hand and that can be touched by the DJ in the course of his work, any equipment casings, microphones and mic stands. The electrical installations in every club will have some sort of trip system fitted so, in theory at least, before enough current leaks to harm any one, the circuit should have tripped out.

The mobile DJ has a slightly different set of problems. In most cases the dangers are similar, but there is an added hazard of not quite knowing how good the circuit is that he has just plugged into; what else is on that circuit and whether that circuit has protection. To be honest, how many mobile DJs are going to roll up for a gig and ask to inspect the venue's distribution board? So it might be a good idea to include a circuit breaker for the equipment, as part of the rig.

Another hazard that exists for the mobile DJ is at a venue where there is a three phase supply. If for some reason the DJ connects his equipment across phases i.e. takes power for some of his equipment from one phase and power for the rest from

Tip

Never remove the earth connection from a mains plug.

another, he could potentially be creating a circuit between two phases. Four hundred and forty volts at 20 amps, could be on the way down the mic stand into that soft fleshy conductive thing holding it. A very good rule of thumb is take all power from one outlet. This also reduces the chances of creating an earth loop.

Earth loops and the resulting phenomena, known as earth hums, are less common nowadays, they too can result as a consequence of taking power for common equipment from more than one mains source. An old remedy used to be ripping open plugs and pulling out the earth connections. Under no circumstances is this to be done. If you are using a big sophisticated rig, you will activate the ground lift circuit. On a smaller PA you should reorganize your mains supply so that all your needs are met from the one outlet.

Another potential hazard for both club and mobile DJs is trailing cables. Usually, for the club DJ these are to be found in his box and the only danger is to him and not to the public.

Hazards to the public

For the mobile DJ, setting up wherever, the potential hazards are a lot greater. You must take all reasonable care to tidy your wiring up and keep it away from your adoring public. If you have to run a cable along the floor, anywhere where it could be accessed by a member of the public, you must ensure that it is at least securely taped down. The roll of gaffa tape included in your toolbox is just for this purpose. Use only good quality, preferably soft, rubber-coated cable for your main power feed, make sure it is 13amp rated, it is not worn or split and that there is nothing showing outside the plugs or sockets other than the coated cable. Use rubber plugs and sockets. They are less likely to crack when thrown down on the floor or trodden on.

Do your speaker, or lighting stands stick out, could someone trip over them, these are questions you need to ask yourself. It is your responsibility to protect the public, they are quite happy to fall over something you didn't warn them about then sue you. You must assess all the hazards associated with what you do, and minimize them, and warn the public of potential hazards such as loudness in close proximity of the speakers (see 'Hearing' below). Do not allow members of the public access to behind the turntables, or any area where they can do themselves and your equipment damage. If you have to, cordon, or screen it off.

Hearing

Relevant to both the DJ and his crowd, is the issue of hearing damage. There are guidelines for exposure levels to loud music over a sustained period, these exist to protect hearing. Since being a DJ relies heavily on that particular sense being fairly good, the DJ must take steps to protect his own hearing. If a resident DJ is a top liner, working 4 nights a week, 6 hours a night, doing doubles and trebles and then hanging out down the studio or the record shop, it won't be long before hearing damage starts. A good reason to wear sound level reducing earplugs, or closed type headphones that are comfortable and light (and keep them on even when not cueing up the next track), is to control the volume to which the ears are exposed. Similarly it might be good if you have a booth monitor speaker setup to keep the

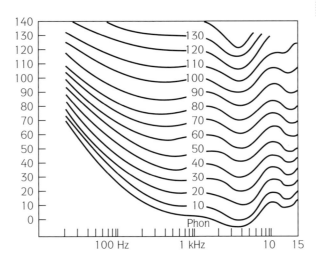

140
130
120
110
100
90
80
70
60
50
40
30
20
10
0

130
120
110
100
90
80
70
60
50
40
30
20
10

Phon

100 Hz   1 kHz   10   15

Figure 8.01
Frequency response of a human ear (equal loudness contours).

level reasonable, your ears are your trade after all. For the crowd, you need to be aware of safe levels. Some clubs will be fitted with noise limiters, which will measure SPL (Sound Pressure Level), either A weighted or, in the case of an acoustic problem, C weighted. The output is limited to the maximum recommended by the current health and safety regulations.

The trouble is that our brains compensate for our environment automatically. In a quiet area our sense of hearing is heightened and we really can hear a pin drop. In a loud environment we are anaesthetised; what was really loud when we first walked into a room now, a few minutes later, sounds OK, and it is here where the danger lies. Our ears also have a built in EQ system. The chart below shows the ear's frequency response curve, which is heightened between 2 to 4 kHz – exactly where a female scream or the cries of a baby fall.

As well as having an in-built EQ, our brains will automatically filter things out that are somehow too pervasive. Many a time I have gone into a place where I have thought, 'boy that treble's a bit sharp', only to notice 15 minutes later that the treble appears to have been cut. Of course it hasn't been, my brain has EQ'd it out for me, automatically. Now I'm thinking, at my age my treble hearing has diminished considerably, so what must the same sound be doing to that 18-year-old right under the speakers?

This is one of the reasons why real time/spectrum analyzers are used to measure frequencies, because our brains will fool us. Similarly, instruments are used to measure sound pressure levels because they are objective. I use a Realistic sound level meter to check the volume in my environments, objectively, for my and my clients' safety, and I would suggest that you do the same. Exposure to a constant level of noise over around 80dB for any length of time can cause permanent hearing damage.

Tinnitus is one result of over exposure to loud noise, it is a ringing in the ears and is a sensation I have often endured. The worst bout I had lasted 4 days and whilst it was not the result of a club or music sound system, I have to tell you it really scared me. It can develop and stay forever.

The ears are a wondrous piece of human engineering and are not to be abused. As you get older your hearing deteriorates anyway, you lose definition at the high

Figure 8.02
Sound level and exposure times before hearing damage occurs. Each 3dB increase represents a doubling of the volume.

Figure 8.03
Chart showing age related hearing loss.

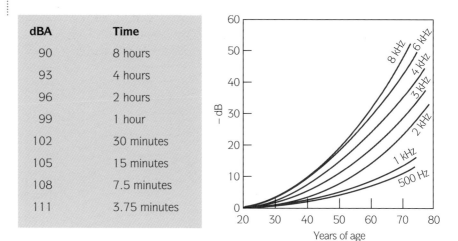

dBA	Time
90	8 hours
93	4 hours
96	2 hours
99	1 hour
102	30 minutes
105	15 minutes
108	7.5 minutes
111	3.75 minutes

end of the frequency spectrum. Figure 8.03 shows the effect of that condition. It has been shown that people who live in a naturally quiet environment suffer a lower rate of hearing loss with age.

We DJs do not live in a naturally quiet environment, so therefore it would stand to reason that we need to be more careful than most. Ears are very easily damaged and very hard, if not impossible, to repair. Without them you have no job, therefore it is up to you to rest them and look after them and to do the same for your audience.

Security

Something that happens less now, with the advent of CCTV, is the DJ policing the club. Invariably from his vantage point in the DJ box, the DJ has a better view of certain parts of the club than anyone else. The standing brief will be, either in code or in plain language, to call security to any incidents which might occur, so a degree of observance on behalf of the DJ is an asset. (So is the ability to lip read and communicate with gestures, especially when gagging and needing someone to supply a drink).

In the unlikely event that a bomb scare is notified, you become the captain of the ship, it is your job to ensure that all your passengers are safely evacuated before you leave. It may be a hoax started by someone who has been refused entry, but when the bomb squad turn up with body armour and sniffer dogs, a certain realization dawns. The chances of this happening are of course, very small, but I personally have had to supervise an evacuation on three occasions.

No matter how much your ego needs massaging, never let anybody interfere with or have a go on your gear, or the gear of which you have temporary custody. Unless that person has a genuine right to touch or access your gear, or you are happy and confident in their ability, keep them away, they will break something or they will hurt themselves, it's so much simpler just to say no.

So being a DJ is not all sweetness and light, there can be a lot more to think about than 'what do I play next?' if you have a job, or 'how am I going to get a job?' if you don't. You really do need to be aware of much more than just the music part. The DJ actually has a lot of power and control and it is important that this power and control is exerted with due consideration for the health and safety of others, which is another reason why his faculties should not be impaired by alcohol or drugs.

Career progression

Radio

Hospital radio or other closed-in, pseudo radio stations, like university stations, are always looking for volunteers. It's one thing working a crowd, be it in a club or at a party, it's a whole other ball game being cheerful talking to magnolia woodchip. Nevertheless, the experience is valuable and will usually be enough to let you know whether or not you could cut it in the real radio world.

There are a lot of radio stations around and they are looking for talent, the better you are when you arrive, the better they like it. Working hospital radio, where you can't hear the end result of your labours, is quite scary but it also teaches you all about levels and gain structure. With no audio to guide you, apart from what's in your cans, suddenly those meters and LEDs start to have meaning.

Don't be kidded that it is an easy option, if you have the aptitude it could well be, again it is a discipline that you have to learn.

To get into hospital radio, go down to your local hospital, find the notice board that tells you all about their radio station and follow the instructions.

Making an audition tape

You will probably be required to send in an audition tape/Mini- Disc™/CD, do it as professionally as you can. Remember this is a hospital, they don't necessarily want a 74 minute mix CD. In fact they will be more interested in listening to you than the music you play. Since all radio is based on split second timing, a good tape will start with an introduction, with you saying your name and contact details and perhaps a little bit about yourself. You might then say the programme will be a 15 minute one, which will start in 10 seconds. That will be followed by 10 seconds of silence and then the programme will start. The people auditioning you don't want to listen to a 1 hour audition tape, which consists of you playing 17 three-minute recordings and linking them with nine minutes of chat. They would rather listen to a 15 minute audition tape, with you playing 20–30 second extracts from tracks and linking those together with nine minutes of chat. After all, the only difference in doing that and doing it for real is the extra time it takes to get to the next link or segment. Don't for one minute think that you just have to sit there and talk inanely for nine minutes. That isn't it at all, what you are doing is just cutting down on the needle time to condense a one-hour show into 15 minutes. When the 15 minutes are up you will stop. They will instinctively check your time, this is radio,

Info

Working in hospital radio will train you to use the inflexion in your voice and train you in the art of phrasing and sounding happy.

where a second of dead air sounds like a lifetime. If you have started and finished on time you will be halfway there.

Working in hospital radio will train you to use the inflexion in your voice and train you in the art of phrasing and sounding happy. You will also learn how to make jingles and the delights of working to no one but yourself. Every so often a message will come from one of the patients, thanking you for brightening up their day, then you will understand why you are there and all the time you thought you were practising to be a star.

The art of the DJ

So far in this book we have concentrated mainly on the physical aspects of Djing, method and methodology and procedures. Whilst I was writing the book I had a conversation with someone about DJing and was asked a simple question. How do you know what to play and when, how does the DJ, on a good night, have the crowd eating out of the palm of his hand and what happens when it all goes pear shaped? Well the answer depends to a degree on whether you are a club or dance DJ or a mobile DJ, but it is ostensibly the same, it's about timing.

For the club DJ the music builds, starting off at a certain level and taking the crowd on a musical ride to a musical high. On the journey the mix of music will be those tunes that are guaranteed to fill the floor, mixed in with cutting edge new tunes and some old favourites not too cheesy but just so good that every so often they are resurrected to fill the groove. Some nights this mix will work like magic, on another night exactly the same running order won't work at all.

Know your audience

The art of being a DJ is looking at that dance floor, looking at that crowd and predicting where to start and which route the musical journey should take on that particular night. Not being so rigid as to say I'm playing this set and that's it, and not so pliable as to resort to safe tunes that anyone could play. Needless to say there are DJ's who are so gifted in this regard that it doesn't matter what they play – it's right, it's good, and it's appropriate for the crowd, the atmosphere, the club, the night, even the time of the night. Why? Well it's a combination of their musical taste and the ability to read the situation and apply what it is in their record box to it; these are the club DJ's who earn the big money.

With the mobile DJ the situation is probably harder because he has no hard and fast rules regarding cutting edge music or genre in which to slot his crowd. Every job is different, there is usually a mixture of age groups, tastes and requirements to fulfil, everything from The Birdie Song, to the underground jazz fusion mix of Bob the Builder. So the situation is harder to call because the mobile DJ has probably got to set up a number of musical journeys which have all got to be taken in the same night to make it a success. So not only has he got to judge several different criteria such as era, style etc. but he also has to tailor the start of each individual journey to the needs of that segment of the crowd. Even geographical origin comes into to play; a southern crowd will not have the same musical requirements as a

Info

The art of being a DJ is looking at that dance floor, looking at that crowd and predicting where to start and which route the musical journey should take on that particular night.

northern crowd and so it goes on. A crowd who are predominantly from Birmingham will want something different from a crowd who are predominantly from Carlisle.

No good playing for the over 40's at 6:30pm in the evening or 1:00am the following morning; don't play the heavy metal thrash right after the buffet and so on. The number of popular records that have been released since say 1961 is in the tens, if not hundreds of thousands. From these, the mobile DJ has to select what is going to do the job that particular night and have people clamouring for his card when he has finished.

In this scenario the mobile DJ has the harder job, there is no way that a template can be fitted over a mobile DJ's function to guarantee success. He could do three jobs, which on the surface are all the same, in one week and they would not even remotely resemble each other. What goes down a storm on one night bombs on the next, the only sure fire tip I can give you is that there will always be certain newish records that everybody irrespective of age or background like, when in trouble revert to those. The trouble you have is figuring out what those are and as always the list changes depending on the year.

It has to said the easiest job is that of specialist DJs, those who play within a tightly restricted genre or time frame and are acknowledged experts in their field. Their crowd knows them, wants to be there and knows what to expect, especially if it's a nostalgia thing.

So there you have it, the art of the DJ is playing the right track at the right time, the variables involved in that simple action are immense and that is where the art really is. Anyone can learn about gain structure and which button to press, it's what happens when the button is pressed that's important.

Doing it for real
by James Camm

11

Hi my name is James Camm. Firstly I am going to tell you about me and my music career and then I'm going to tell you how I managed to do it and try and give you a few pointers into helping your career. This is not a sure fire way to get to the top of the DJing ladder, but just a guide of things that some people do not know about or forget about.

I am 24 and have been DJing for 10 years. I was tutored on all aspects of being a DJ by the author of this book, Charlie Slaney. Over those 10 years of DJing I have done more than most can imagine.

I was asked to play at a friend's birthday party at his house; it was here I met Jon Hill, a promoter of a big club night called Golden which was based in Manchester and Stoke on Trent. I gave him a CD and thought nothing more of it. I later received a phone call and asked if I would like to go to Creamfields as a fill in DJ. This was my first ever gig out side of the bedroom and it was at Creamfields in the Golden Arena. As luck would have it the first DJ was a no show and I was thrown in at the deep end and played nervously to over 10,000 people. Jon was impressed by my set and I was offered my first residency at Golden's flagship club in Stoke on Trent playing alongside the world's biggest DJs. It wasn't long before things really started to move in the right direction.

After three months playing at Golden I was asked by Bacardi to play an event at the Brighton Centre to help launch their new drink: Bacardi Breezer. I played alongside US house Legend Todd Terry to 5000 people. From the publicity of the event I was booked to play my first club abroad. I headlined at 'Zillion' clubs in Antwerp, Belgium and I then jumped on a plane straight after the event to return to the UK to play at Golden's 8th birthday alongside Sasha, Carl Cox and Paul Van Dyke which was broadcast live on BBC Radio one's Essential Mix.

One day while shopping for records I met a guy by the name of Oliver Straughan. We swapped CDs with each other and found our musical tastes were similar. This was to be the start of a great recording career together. Under the name Oliver James we have produced tracks and re-mixes for Serious Records, Good:as Records and Redemption. Our tracks have received airplay on BBC Radio 1 and London's Kiss FM. Our tracks have also received plays from Judge Jules, Lisa Lashes, Scott Project, Rob Tissera and Graham Gold but to name a few.

Making music boosted my career tenfold; people who had never heard of James Camm now knew who I was and what I played. At a weekend I was playing two gigs a night, sometimes even three.

I started getting bookings to play the UK's biggest festivals including V2004 (which I have now played for the past four years) and Ministry Of Sound at Knebworth alongside chart topping Jamiroqui. I also started to get a lot more bookings to play abroad. I clocked up a lot of air miles playing a tour of Asia which included Kuala Lumpur and Hong Kong. This tour was reviewed by Simon Morrison and featured in DJ Magazine in 2003. On the back of this tour I was booked to headline at huge New Year's Eve beach party in Dubai. I played under a moonlit beach to 5000 people. This is my fondest DJing memory to date.

Practice makes perfect

In the 70's and 80's everyone wanted to be in a band and the guitar was the biggest selling instrument of the time. In today's day and age the guitar has moved over to the decks. Today young people don't want to be in a band they want to be a DJ. I have literally met thousands of clubbers who have decks but one thing makes the real DJs stand out from the rest. Practice!

Once you have got your equipment and a hand full of records the next step is probably one of the hardest the longest. I find DJing very easy but only because I put so much time into practising. For some people they find the whole concept daunting and if they can't do it after a few weeks they give up. If this is you then please stick with it, it's so rewarding when you get the hang of it. For three straight years I spent every night in my room with my decks practising for roughly three hours.

Once you have the hang of beat mixing, cutting and scratching this doesn't mean you are ready to be a working DJ. You have to practise and after time you will begin to develop your own particular style. Every time I would mix I would record the session, this would then allow me to go back and listen to the mistakes I had made, so I recommend this very much. When listening to yourself mix when you actually doing it live it's easy to think to yourself what you are hearing is very good, but record yourself, listen back and I promise you will be able to hear mistakes. To get another opinion, record one of you sessions and maybe give it to a friend or another DJ and ask them for advice or some input into your mixing. If they do have any criticism don't take it the wrong way; they may have a point, listen back to your stuff and see how you can improve.

OK so you've got decks, you can mix, now what's the next step to get to play a club? Self promotion! Self promotion! Self promotion. I cannot state it enough; people won't come looking for you. Only you can help yourself to make a career in the DJing industry.

Record a mix CD

A mix CD is a very important tool in getting your style and technical ability heard by all sorts of people. I used to record one CD every month so that my style was always sounding fresh and new. Remember when you record it try and make it a full hour and don't just put all the latest records on; it's your style that will get you a gig, not the biggest dance anthems out of the top 40. Once you've recorded your CD don't worry about making too many copies. Send them to club nights, local bars, other DJs, your mates and your mates' mates. You never know where that cd is gonna end up. The idea of a CD is to get a buzz going about yourself and people talking about you, and friends are a good way of achieving this and if all of your friends are driving around in their car with your CD coming out of their speakers it won't be long until you're playing your mates next house party. Also carry a CD with you, everywhere you go, you never know who you are going to bump into and you always want a cd at the ready. A really important thing to remember is always to put your name and contact details on the CD. The number of CDs I have received and I really liked but couldn't contact the guy is unbelievable. Simply write your email address on it or a mobile number.

When you have recorded a good mix cd and you are happy with it, consider sending it into competitions such as radio comps or magazine comps. BBC Radio 1 DJ Yousef was a Bedroom Bedlam winner in Music magazine. He went from playing in his room to becoming a very big and successful DJ because of this competition. For the price of a stamp what have you got to lose?

The internet

One of the best things I ever did to help my career was to set up my own website to help self promotion. It doesn't have to be anything fancy, just a little bit about yourself, an online mix and a few photos. And don't forget your contact details. A website is great because it allows people from all over the world to check you out and what you do. You don't have to spend a fortune on your website. Everyone has a friend or knows someone who makes websites. My first one was very basic but as my career moved up the ladder I updated my site which contained everything from forthcoming gigs, a diary of my latest gigs, online mixes, interviews with other big named DJs, and competitions. And every so often I would do live web casts. At one point I had over 1500 members on my site who were all reading or listening to what I was up to. This was fantastic self promotion. Clubbing message boards are also a great way of meeting people and self promoting yourself. I know a lot of promoters, DJs and industry bods who use message boards for different reasons but you never know who you are going to meet or end up talking to. Don't just use the internet to say you are the greatest DJ in the world. Get talking to people, swap mix tapes and make contacts. Through the internet I have established contact with people who have subsequntly offered me gigs.

Mailing lists

Mailing lists are a great way of getting free records and getting them months before they are released to the general public. Mailing lists aren't as easy to get on to because to qualify you have to be a working DJ playing in front of a good crowd of people at least once a week. If you are, then great. All the gigs you play at save some flyers with your name on and keep them, they will come in very useful later on. The next step is to contact the record labels you like or are playing most of, these details can usually be found on the sleve notes of a 12 inch or sometimes on the record itself. A simple email or phone call to the label manager telling him who you are, where you play and to how many people you are playing to and that you would are playing a lot of their records and that you would like to get onto their mailing list. This will be probably be the hardest part of getting on the list but once you do it will be worth it. You will have to prove to them why you should receive their records for free. Ideally you need to think about your reply. Saying you play to over 5000 people every week at your local super club won't help either. Every label will want proof of who you are and what you say is true. This is where those flyers from all your previous gigs come in, send them photocopies of these flyers along with another press cuttings etc to support your case. It won't harm either to send them a current CD of yourself along with business card and a photo of yourself. Think about it, who are they going to put on the list – someone who rings up and asks to be put on the list, or someone who rings up and sends loads of information about their DJing credentials.

A lot of record companies use promotional companies to operate their mailing lists. Two that were very useful for me were Power Promotions and Hyperactive. Their job is to take a record and distribute a few hundred copies to select DJs on their database to try and create a hype. The DJs then sent back a reaction sheet on what they thought of the tune and the reaction of the crowd to it. This allows them to go back to record companies with their findings and the record company then decides whether to release it or not.

Once you get onto a mailing list there are several things which you have to do in order to stay on the list. The first thing is to always fill in the reaction sheets honestly and return them on time. Secondly you must do a weekly chart which is basically a list of the top 20 records you are playing that week. Your chart must then be faxed back to them and then faxed to a list of numbers they will give you including magazines, record labels etc. Failing to do these two things will see you being thrown off the mailing list very quickly. Remember there are thousands of DJs out there who would love to be on a mailing list.

One thing that is tempting to DJs that cannot get onto a mailing list is to download music from illegal websites. I am totally against obtaining music in this manner. Also nightclubs and bars have now become targets for raids by authorities looking for DJs playing pirated music. You can be fined thousands of pounds for every downloaded track you have. Is it really worth saving a few pounds at the record shop?

Playing your first gig

OK so you've recorded your mix CD, and sent it to DJ agencies, bar owners and club promoters and one day you get a call offering you a gig. Depending on where it is you have a number of options on how to play your set. Here I'm going to explain the different sets you should play depending on the gig.

Playing a pre- club bar

If the gig you have been offered is in a bar then chances are you will be playing all night. This may be a long set of up to four hours, so the idea here is to pace yourself. For example the bar probably won't get full until 9 pm so don't play all your biggest records before your crowd gets there. The records you play should also be a bit more commercial because chances are the crowd you're playing to will not have heard of the dirty underground white label you think is great. You're being paid to keep the bar full, so play the tracks the crowd have heard of. You are there to entertain everyone there, not just yourself so don't just play your favourite records, try to judge the crowd. If they aren't dancing to something, change the style slightly. If they start singing along to a vocal track then play more vocal tracks. The art of DJing is all about watching the crowd and knowing what to play next. Playing in a bar you will also get a lot of requests. You don't have to play what they request but if it will fit in with what you are playing and you haven't already played it then give it a spin.

Playing a club

Chances are if this is your first club gig that you will be playing the warm up set. By this I mean you will be playing the first hour before the big DJs arrive. There are rules that you have to follow when playing the warm up set because you can't go banging it out with the biggest tunes of the moment. The promoter wants you to warm the crowd up, they are paying the big boys to fire it up. Secondly if the big DJ who is on after you turns up and you are playing all the tunes he was going to play he won't be happy. He has a lot of power and chances are you won't play that club again. So remember, warming up means taking it easy, you may have to alter your style slightly but try and get a feel for the crowd on the dance floor and build it up slowly towards the end of your set. It is also helpful if you find out who is spinning after you. If you know what sort of style they play you have a marker of what you can play up to, but also what you can't step over.

Playing warm up sets is nothing to get disheartened about, for one it is good practice for you playing in front of crowds, people will start recognising you and your style, building up a fan base and it will only be a matter of time before you are asked to play that peak time set you have been waiting for.

Being a good DJ

Here are just a few little pointers into being a good professional working DJ.

- Never pay money to play no matter how desperate you are to be a DJ. There are a lot of conmen out there who like to take advantage of wannabe DJs.
- When starting out never put any gig beneath you. I was offered a small house party for a mate's birthday; I did it and met a big club promoter at the party.
- Never promise what you can't deliver and always keep your word.
- Always turn up at every gig you have been booked for.
- Avoid alcohol and drugs. If you take either when playing it will certainly affect your performance. Club promoters pay you to entertain the customers and not to make a fool of yourself behind the decks.
- Never slag anybody off. If you are asked your opinion about another DJ make sure what comes out of your mouth is praise. If you can't praise them don't say anything. Slagging people off only makes you look bad and will not help with your career.

I hope that what I have written will be of some use to you. Remember DJing is also about fun and enjoying yourself, so live it, and you never know you may see me on the dance floor.

DJ James Camm by author Charles Slaney

My thanks to James Camm for his kind words, what he rather modestly doesn't tell you that he is a very nice guy, in spite of having been and done what he has done he remains very ordinary and very grounded. What he also doesn't tell you, or rather hides beneath the 'then I did this' is of the focus and work he put into getting to his goals. I can honestly say that he worked far harder in his career than I ever did. When I say harder I mean that, as a young teenager, to learn microphone technique he called bingo as a summer job and then he ploughed all his earnings into records, then samplers, sequencers etc. To get into clubs to watch people work he would sell glo sticks and other paraphernalia sell em quick and then find a spot beside the DJ box where he could see what went on.

He never turned a booking down that was within his expertise, and as you read, it was at a house party that he got picked up, that and the fact he was already a well known face in the clubs, and in the record shops, and a nice guy got him started. His protégé, if I can use that word did her first essential mix on Radio 1 in October 2005. Not that he would tell you himself that he had anything to do with it. The other thing he doesn't tell you is how he could earn £1000 extra on a night while selflessly promoting the next gig. How? Well I'll tell you, by producing a licensed mix of the night accompanied with photos from inside the event selling at £10.00 each, and advertising the next event. Say 2000 people attend 10% buy the CD you do the maths. As I write this I'm listening to one recorded at the Fat Cat Café in Stoke on the 17th June 2004.

James is also actively involved in hands on training at some Universities and Community initiatives that run DJ courses. If you see one that has his name attached it would be well worth taking a look. PS his full name is Dominic James Camm, or DJ Camm how spooky is that?

Copyright and licensing

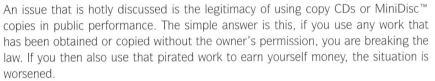

An issue that is hotly discussed is the legitimacy of using copy CDs or MiniDisc™ copies in public performance. The simple answer is this, if you use any work that has been obtained or copied without the owner's permission, you are breaking the law. If you then also use that pirated work to earn yourself money, the situation is worsened.

All establishments, which have a licence for music and dancing, will pay some kind of licence fee in respect of the copyrights that they use in giving a music performance. The organisations that administer those licences in the UK for differing establishments are the PRS (Performing Right Society) and the PPL (Phonographic Performance Ltd). If you play, using legally obtained copyright material, in such establishments, you will be covered under a blanket licence payment, made to one of these two organizations. If the event is a wedding or birthday party, then it is not deemed to be a public event, it is deemed to be a domestic event, so according to the PPL no licence for that specific event is necessary.

Back to plain old copyright. This is quite important; we are going to see, in the next couple of years, a drastic alteration in what club DJs, in particular, play. I am convinced that the DJ will remix the shop-bought tune to suit his requirements and that the copyright artist will in fact become a raw material supplier. Does this adaptation of an original work infringe copyright?

My opinion is that it does not. In the same way that introducing a loop, pressing a flange button or altering the EQ whilst a track is playing does not impinge on the copyright owner's rights, neither will swapping the track around, putting bits through filters and generally altering the piece's dynamics. If however, the DJ were to market that as his work and sell a product based on it, as opposed to playing sound waves, without reaching an agreement with the copyright owner, then that would be an infringement of the copyright.

It is very easy in a digital age to buy a DAT machine or MiniDisc™ and record MTV's digital output, edit it and then play it. The temptation is great. So is the temptation to download MP3s from the Internet and convert those to CDs. However, I personally believe many (past) musicians have been sidelined by mainstream society for long enough, their talents ignored, their greatness lost. Thus, modern musicians don't need us stealing their work.

To copy work, with the intent of depriving the owners of income in order that you can make more income, isn't right. We are not talking about making a tape of someone else's CD to listen to in the car although even that's illegal. We are talk-

Info

If you use any work that has been obtained or copied without the owner's permission, you are breaking the law.

ing about using someone else's music to make you money, without you having paid for it in the first place.

The artists get little enough already and although you could use the argument quite convincingly, that it's not them, but the retailer and record company you are depriving of income, in reality the artist suffers. So don't do it. You are not covered by any licensing arrangement to play pirated music.

Be assured, if you are tempted to use pirate CDs or MiniDiscs™, the authorities have the power not only to prosecute you, but also to seize the equipment you used. Computers, CD Recorders, CD originals, CD Players, mixers, amplifiers, satellite equipment, van, cuddly toy, set of sliding doors, get the picture, they like to make an example of you and if you are caught they will.

For more information on licensing issues see:

- Performing Right Society (PRS)
  29-33 Berners Street, London W1T 3AB
  Tel: 020 7580 5544. www.prs.co.uk
- Phonographic Performance Ltd. (PPL)
  1 Upper James Street, London W1F 9DE
  Tel: 020 7534 1000. www.ppluk.com
- MCPS-PRS Alliance
  Copyright House
  29-33 Berners Street
  London W1T 3AB
  Tel: 020 7580 5544. www.mcps.co.uk
  The MCPS is in partnership with the PRS, but is a separate autonomous organization, which exists to collect royalties on behalf of musicians and composers from radio stations and the like. It is also instrumental in granting rights between users for specific pieces of music.

If you get to the next stage of the business and become a music producer, you will need to clear samples and suchlike and you may wish to register with the MCPS, in order that you are paid royalties when your music is played.

DJ products

13

DMC, Music Factory and CD Pool

DMC

The Disco Mix Club (DMC) was kicked off in 1983 by Tony Prince, who was already a well known, respected and established Radio Luxembourg DJ and then programme controller. Until 1982, mix records were made by cover artists imitating the originals and singing a medley of the songs segued into one. Then in March 1982, a young trainee barrister called Alan Coulthard sent a beat mix he made called 'The Solar Symphony', featuring the original artists, to Tony Prince at Radio Luxembourg. At around the same time, he also sent Tony Prince the now famous 'Kool & The Gang Megamix'.

Tony, ever the innovator – (and it needs to be said, he is a real advocate of the importance of the DJ, who always looks for an innovative way to advance the role of the DJ in public consciousness) realized that the megamix, as it was to become known, could be an extremely useful DJ resource. As a result of airplay, the Coulthard mixes as presented by Tony Prince attracted a great deal of attention. So in February 1983, the Disco Mix Club was born and the era of microphone presentation was about to give way to the mix.

The DMC gave the world the first Dance/DJ orientated magazine Mixmag and it was instrumental in setting up the Disco Mix Championships. It produces a range of DJ products and was instrumental in the changes that resulted in the DJ/Dance industry that we have today. Tony Prince took the DJ from presenter to innovator, and he was probably as important in the evolution of the modern DJ as Jimmy Savile was to the existence of the DJ in the first place.

The DMC can be found on the Internet at www.dmcworld.com or, tel: 01628 667124. Amongst a host of other things, they offer a subscription based pre-release monthly CD, similar to the products available from the CD Pool, which have some important tracks that subscribers get first.

Music Factory

The Music Factory Mastermixes are every mobile DJ's best friend, if you are a working mobile DJ you will have a Mastermix CD or four in your box. You could conceivably present a 4 hour party using only their products and touch on every genre of musical taste. They have a vast range of both occasion based and contemporary based products. Like the DMC, they have been around for a while but

Websites

DMC
www.dmcworld.com

Music Factory
www.mastermixdj.com

CD Pool
www.cdpool.co.uk

Info

Music Factory Mastermix
Hawthorne House
Fitzwilliam Street,
Parkgate, Rotherham,
South Yorks, S62 6EP, UK
Tel 0870 7772650
www.mastermixdj.com

unlike the DMC they don't seem to get involved in the cutting edge stuff, their bread and butter is the party oriented mobile DJ. Their repertoire is large and very useful and it is well worth a glance through the catalogue. I guarantee you will, if you are serious in your intent to be a mobile DJ, buy and use some Mastermix products.

CD Pool

The CD Pool is another subscription-based organization. It was originally called The Pioneer CD Pool and was kicked off to coincide with the release of the now ubiquitous Pioneer DJ series CD equipment in the mid-90s. In those days, dance based music was limited to vinyl; the CD Pool got those dance based tracks, the full 12 inch mixes, onto CD. As the genres diversified, so did they, and now they offer a range of subscription based monthly CDs for most of the genres you will come across. They even do a classic dance collection as well. As well as CDs the CD Pool now do equipment, at discounted rates for members. Check them out at www.cdpool.com

Software

There is lot of DJ user friendly software available on the market, from loop based composition programs like E Jay to fully fledged loop plus midi, plus kitchen sink programs like Acid, right across the spectrum to MP3 jukeboxes and mixing systems. The merits of individual programs comprise a vast subject area, which will make another book. The cutting edge producer DJ or musician will probably already be up to speed with Emagic Logic or Pro Tools or Cool Edit Pro, Cubase or Cakewalk. If you are not a cutting edge producer, but are interested in enhancing and expanding what you do, read on.

This section is not so much about music creation programs, but mixing programs. Why, because although CDs are lighter than vinyl and easy to carry round, why carry 400 CDs, when 100 will do and still contain all the music needed? How many times are all the tracks on a shop-bought CD used? The answer is never. In the same way the Mastermixers do compilation party CDs, anyone with a computer, the right software and a CD Writer can do the same.

Obviously, to use software, a computer is needed. The better the computer, the faster it does everything. Having said that most modern computers are up to the task. One bit of advice though is get a decent soundcard, (external if you use a laptop) there are lots about, people in the know seem to recommend M Audio products, I was recommended one, and it is excellent, it doesn't clip as easily as a 'normal' sound card.

Once the computer is in place, software is needed, but which ones? The good news is that demo versions of most software are available and finding them isn't that difficult. There is a magazine called Computer Music which comes with a cover CD ROM containing demos of all sorts of useful music programs. I found Acid here. The Internet sites of the software manufactures will also have trial downloads of the program, either one that doesn't allow the saving of the work, or that has reduced features, or perhaps it is a full version on a time limit. This is one reason why an active Internet connection is recommended.

PCs, unlike Apple Macs, are prone to crash, and you run the risk of losing data.

There are two ways that the impact of this inevitable PC characteristic can be lessened. Firstly, have two hard drives installed, or a least one large hard drive, partitioned to behave as two: one drive or partition is for the operating system and programs, the other is for data. When the PC crashes, it is usually as a result of something going awry in the operating system or a program. The C drive or partition is where these live, so it will just be the C drive that needs re formatting, the data stored on the other drives, D and E (if there are 3), will be intact and useable.

The second precaution is to store all downloaded programs or upgrades where the original disks do not exist, on a written CD. That way, when the PC crashes, the downloaded programs are just reloaded in the same way as all the other programs are loaded, from a disk. By keeping an 'open' CD to hand, the disk can just be topped up as and when necessary, from the downloads' folder, until it is full, then it is finalized in the normal manner.

My first-ever piece of primitive computer mixing was using Adobe Premiere 4.2LE, which is actually a video editing program that just happens to contain a couple of stereo tracks. There was a tool to control the volume of those tracks between designated points and a drag and drop facility to within a frame (1/25th second). There was even a way of speeding up or slowing down the track, but the pitch alterations were very noticeable. For beat mixing, where the beats are exact, or chop mixing, or fade in and out, it was OK. It was 'bundled' software, i.e. it was free with a piece of hardware.

The newer programs allow for time stretching and tempo alterations, whilst maintaining the original pitch. The sophisticated ones, like Acid, allow the use of MIDI files along with sample loops in the creation of a finished piece. The end result of all this is to enable the user to program a set of music containing several different tracks, or bits of different tracks, to suit the user's purposes and then burn that onto a CD.

Without being specific, below is a list of the types of programs that are needed and useable as DIY tools, for self made compilation albums.

CD-DA converter (CD ripper)

A piece of software that extracts the audio information from a CD and puts it onto the hard drive as a .wav file. Very often, this is bundled with the CD Writer or maybe Soundcard hardware, it is what is known as a utility program. Avoid the ones that use compression.

Wave editor

This is a piece of software that allows manipulation of the .wav file by an edit or by chopping it up into loops. Again, this can come as a utility bundled with a Soundcard. Some are very basic, some are not. Sound Forge from Sonic Foundry is probably the de facto interim standard, which falls between being basic and super specified. It is very good, it contains a lot of facilities and plug ins, such as effects and noise reduction and EQ which are easily used.

Mixing program

This is quite a difficult piece of software to define because any program that allows the playing of two or more stereo files at the same time could conceivably be a mixing program. Whereas a wave editor allows the manipulation of the .wav file of a

Info

When downloading large files from the Internet, use a download monitor like GoZilla. If for some reason the connection is broken before the download is finished, GoZilla allows the resumption from where the break occurred, rather than having to start again.

stereo source, a mixing program allows for the combination (two or more) of those .wav files (stereo sources) in a creative fashion. A loop here, a section there, a bit of another piece over there. Not surprisingly there are a few available, Acid is among the numerous candidates. The Mix Meister is another mixing program available by download. (This calculates the bpm of tracks and arranges them in ascending or descending order automatically, all the user has to do is load the folder where the tracks are stored). There are also featured high level programs like Cool Edit Pro.

DA (.wav) – CD converter

The reverse of the very first program. Finally, after it's all been put together, it needs to go back on CD, so that it can be played out in the real world. The program to do this, again, is usually shipped with the CD writer/rewriter.

It has been necessary to generalize here somewhat. Given the rate at which technology moves and new products become available, to do anything other than offer a general overview of the type of programs needed would be counterproductive. As this is being written, there are certain programs that are current and standard, but by the time you are reading it, there could be a whole new set of standards and products available.

In earlier chapters, the point has been made about the DJ's world becoming one where the uniqueness of product will be a DJ's claim to fame; and that it is from manipulating the raw material of providers' music (within a computer) that this uniqueness will arrive. Not only that, for the DJ doing mobile work, wedding receptions, birthday parties etc., how much more efficient he will be creating compilations, which he knows will move his crowd and make his job easier. Certainly, he will have less to carry, lose or damage.

Just before we go. It is interesting to note that the DJ is the broker of new music and new talent from whichever culture, source or location, using whatever technology may be available. He may evolve to be not only the producer, remixer and engineer but also the originator. One thing is certain, the DJ is here to stay.

DJ resources

14

The Internet is a very good source of information for the aspiring DJ.

The following is by no means a definitive list, as there are new sites coming on line all the time, but a list of the sites I have visited in the course of my own activities and in researching the book.

www.adobe.com If you haven't got it already, get a free download of Adobe Acrobat Reader, essential for the PDF files that are used for manuals, brochures and specifications on the net.

www.americandj.com A fantastic site showcasing American DJs' range of superb gear.

www.allen-heath.com and **www.xone.co.uk** Allen & Heath are a pro audio mixer manufacturer with a world wide market and reputation, they would not put their name on a DJ mixer unless it was something special.

www.aphex.com Home page of the Aphex Corporation of Aural Exciter® fame.

www.behringer.de/eng/products/default.htm English homepage of German equipment manufacturer Behringer, whose quality products are not expensive, or as expensive as their much hyped peers.

www.beyerdynamic.co.uk UK homepage of German manufacturer of premier quality headphones and microphones.

www.canford.co.uk Leading UK pro audio and accessories supplier.

www.cdpool.com A subscription based service opened at first as the Pioneer CD Pool to provide pre releases of dance tracks on CD. Now produces a range of CDs covering various genres available on a monthly subscription.

www.citronic.co.uk The first manufacturer of quality separate DJ mixers, probably in the world.

www.cpc.co.uk CPC sell everything electrical and a lot more, a very good source of leads and connectors at reasonable prices. You will use them more than you realize.

www.crownaudio.com The Crown website specs and end uses of all their gear as well as links to AKG, DBX, Dod and other manufacturers.

www.djmag.com A website for a magazine, for club based DJ's.

www.djsounds.com Pioneer site for everything DJ, 'nuff said.

www.dod.com Respected American manufacturer of Graphics and Crossovers and a very good compressor, the 866.

www.ebay.co.uk Go onto the UK site, register there, then go to eBay Germany. Have a look at the second hand equipment on offer.

www.eclerdjdivision.com Ecler homepage.

www.eminence-speaker.com Best known of the not-having-to-sell-a-body-part-to-own-one, speaker manufacturers, good site.

www.formula-sound.com A bespoke UK manufacturer, a bit like a British Ecler. No go faster bits, what you get is what you need and it works very well. Suitably priced to inspire confidence, if they were made anywhere else in the world other than Stockport, you would be selling your bodies to own one.

www.google.com This is a search engine; once you have downloaded and attached it to your IE toolbar, all you need to do is type in the piece of equipment or whatever you are looking for. It will display pages of potential sites that may have the information you need.

www.hblitherland.co.uk A catchall catalogue supplier of quality lighting and audio from Blackpool not all the bits that CPC carry but some high end equipment for Club PA and Mobile use. Trade Only nudge nudge.

www.hkaudio.com The Hughes & Kettner site with details of all their gear.

www.i-dj.co.uk International DJ magazine homepage, reviews on gear and the like are on here along with useful links.

www.kam.co.uk Homepage of DJ Gear manufacturer KAM.

www.loot.com Loads of second hand gear here.

www.magpiedirect.com This is an invaluable source for analogue re masters to CD, their inventory is huge, the site is easy to navigate, the service is excellent and the prices are very competitive.

www.mobilebeat.com Primarily an American based website, specifically for the mobile DJ, lots of resources and links and stuff here.

www.numark.com Numark have certainly made their mark on the DJ industry, with a range of forward thinking and increasingly high profile products.

www.omnitronics.com The Germans are at it again. Omnitronics website is very clean, easy to use and informative. Stunning range and images of product lines, so who needs a shop?

www.peavey.com American manufacturer noted for amplification and speakers.

www.rane.com Established and reputable equipment manufacturer, oozes quality and functionality.

www.raperandwayman.com Leading UK pro audio and accessories supplier.

www.stantonmagnetics.com World famous cartridge and stylus manufacturer, now does turntables, mixers and other bits.

www.studiospares.co.uk Leading UK pro audio and accessories supplier.

www.shure.com American Shure Microphones are the world's best known microphones, with an enviable reputation in key areas, check them out.

www.vestax.co.uk Homepage of well respected and very innovative equipment manufacturer.

Index